David Rhodes was born in Northampton in 1943. His mother died suddenly when he was seven and the family moved north, living for a time in a caravan behind a fish and chip shop in Manchester. Ten schools and three universities have contributed to his education, but he has learned the most important lessons in life from the homeless and marginalized people he has met.

After working as a national newspaper journalist, he was ordained in 1972. In 1994, he joined the ecumenical project Faith in Leeds where he started his innovative 'Retreats on the Streets' to help Christians make the vital connection between their faith and social justice. After several years as chaplain to the Children's Society, he now works as a freelance writer and conference speaker. He is the author of the best-selling *Faith in Dark Places*, *Advent Adventure* and *Lenten Adventure*.

SPARROW STORY

The Gospel for Today

David Rhodes

First published in Great Britain in 2006

Society for Promoting Christian Knowledge
36 Causton Street
London SW1P 4ST

British Library Cataloguing-in-Publication Data
A catalogue record for this book is available from the British Library

ISBN-13: 978-0-281-05790-0
ISBN-10: 0-281-05790-7

1 3 5 7 9 10 8 6 4 2

Typeset by Graphicraft Ltd., Hong Kong
Printed in Great Britain by Bookmarque Ltd., Croydon, Surrey

*Dedicated to all those who endure
poverty, exploitation and oppression:
some of whom have honoured me with their friendship*

Contents

Contents

Contents

A word of warning

Look, I know what you're thinking. You expect a book to be written by someone significant – someone with learning. And what have you got? A bird book. A book about God written by a sparrow. Sparrows that are two a penny, as someone says.

OK, so if you're not happy – go find another book. All I'm telling you is this: I was there. With the Boss and the boys. And Mary the Mags and Petros, alias the Rok, and the guys with the guns, and the rest. I saw what happened. The fun things and the scary things. The drinking and the laughter and the tears.

And then the bad things. The time, early on, when it starts to go wrong. The Robed Ones plotting and scheming and really getting heated up over what the Boss is doing. Over how he challenges their power so their unjust system is threatened. And, in the background, bad people. Like Sly Mammon. And then, worse still, there is the fly.

And how it all suddenly comes apart. And how the Boss seems to let it happen; as though it has to happen. And we think we are all dead and gone. Especially him.

Then what happens afterwards: the confusion and the arguments; the memories and the mystery. And then the counter-attack.

And it's still going on.

So: that's the pitch. And if it's not good enough or safe enough for you, then tough. Go down the pub; turn on the TV; or maybe have yourself a good long sleep. But I'm going to tell the story anyway.

And why am I telling it? Maybe to remember. Maybe so others will know. That they are not alone. That they have meaning. That they are loved.

Strange rumours

Johnny Palotski is definitely dead. Five bullets in the brain and an official autopsy report leave no doubt about that. So how come the guy is still causing such big trouble up and down the land?

Personally, I always got on well with Johnny – which may sound a strange thing for a sparrow to be saying. It all starts off one morning when I notice a paper bag someone has dropped in the street. And what should I find when I go to investigate, but a half-eaten sandwich. So there I am helping myself when suddenly a door opens and this guy shouts: 'Hey, bird. That is my supper you are eating.'

At first I do not understand why someone should leave their supper in the street but then, when I look at this guy's face, I begin to think that maybe he is not entirely sober when he gets home last night. Nor is he likely to want anything but black coffee today. So I reckon it is OK to go on eating his supper.

And that is how it begins. Each day I show up to see what is happening with Johnny Palotski, and each day he throws out some bits of bread in a neighbourly sort of way until, by the time a month has passed, we are getting to know each other quite well.

Then, one day, there is no bread outside his open door. Instead he shouts from inside the house: 'Hey, Monsieur le Wazzo. Why should I go running round after you all the time? From now on if you want breakfast, you come and get it.'

It takes me a day or two to get the hang of this, but before long I am dropping into Johnny's place each morning. He is putting bits of bread on the table for me and we eat together in a companionable silence: not least because Johnny Palotski seems to have a permanent hangover.

But it is no wonder Johnny drinks so much, since life seems tough for the guy. For three years now he is a reporter on the city's newspaper, but Johnny is not very good at his job. This is because he has the unfortunate habit of telling the truth and, in these troubled times, that is not always a helpful thing. Hardly a week goes past but what Johnny is having big arguments at work about the stuff he writes about the Occupation.

Many journalists are embedded with the Army and they write the sort of stories the Army likes to see. But Johnny Palotski is somewhat averse to being told what to write and the only person he is interested in being embedded with is a lady called Liberty Lavender who lives down the street. But this is not likely to happen because, while Liberty Lavender is a fine-looking lady in all respects, she is also very smart. And there is no way a class act like her is going to get involved with a drunk like Johnny Palotski who drops his dinner in the street and talks to the birds.

Then, one day, Johnny does not show up for breakfast. In fact it is well into the afternoon before he is able to get up off the bedroom floor. But maybe a guy is entitled to have a drink or two when he has just been fired from his job. Not that Johnny wasn't asking for it to happen. Even though he knows the paper's policy on the Occupation, he still goes and writes some crazy story.

The story is about a strange rumour that is going round the place. Who starts this rumour, nobody knows. But it does not go away. And one reason it does not go away is that it makes people smile. Which in these days is a most unusual thing: for why should people smile when they live under military occupation and there is great poverty and the hospitals get bombed and the electric and water supplies do not work? And tanks come and smash down people's homes in the night and sometimes people are shot in the street by army snipers.

But now they have started to smile because the rumour is that things are going to change. The army of occupation is going to get thrown out and the people who collude with the Army are going to get put in jail. And there will be a leader who will make all this happen – and maybe it has already begun.

Or maybe all that has begun is Johnny Palotski's early retirement. Which is not such a good thing, especially when you have the rent to pay. But Johnny is not worrying about the rent, because right now he is dying. Lying on the sofa in the untidy living room, his face has gone a strange yellow colour and he is not breathing so good; and it is two days before anyone realizes he is sick.

Had he known what was going on, Johnny Palotski would have been mortified that Liberty Lavender should find him in this state. But on the morning of the third day she shows up at his back door and walks straight in as though she owns the place. Which it turns out that she does.

Two hours later the doctor is checking Johnny over and telling Liberty Lavender that things are not good with this boy. His liver is destroyed by the drink and maybe he will die; and someone must stay with him.

Afterwards people say it is a fine thing Liberty Lavender does, sitting up night and day with this drunk and dabbing his brow and talking kindly to him, even though he is out to the world and cannot hear a thing. Eventually, whether it is being nursed by the lovely Liberty Lavender nobody knows, but against all the odds, Johnny Palotski pulls through.

But after that things are different. Johnny never touches the drink again. And it is round about this time that the leaflets start to appear. Somewhere, someone is running an underground press.

The mysterious leaflets cause great amusement among the people because they talk about the overthrow of the Occupation and an end to the suffering and how the one who will do this is coming. And though most people do not believe the leaflets, they are glad someone has the courage to say these things. Especially as it makes the occupation forces look foolish. And there is little doubt in many people's minds but that Johnny Palotski has a hand in all this.

This thought is also in the minds of the regional administrator and the army colonel who is in charge of this sector. So it should have surprised nobody that one night two jeeps pull up outside Johnny Palotski's home and he is taken away. Looking back I do not think it even comes as a surprise to Johnny himself, for one day when we are having breakfast he suddenly looks up and says:

'Wazzo, my friend. It is time for us to move on. For me it is the end of the story, but for the one who is coming it is only the start. When I was sick I have this dream that Liberty Lavender sits with me and strokes my brow and tells me stories of when we were children and I am so happy I think I am dead and gone to heaven.

'When I come round, she is not there. But I almost think I can smell perfume in the house and the place looks tidier than I can remember it being. But, most of all, Wazzo, my friend, I dream about the one who is coming. Yesterday I think I saw him in the street, this one sent by God. But maybe my brain is on the blink as well as my liver.

'Also, I think other people may be coming and so perhaps I do not need to worry about my liver after all.

'But you need to move out, Wazzo. Go find the stranger I am speaking of. You will not have any trouble, for there will be many people with him.'

Then, two days later, he is gone and I never see him again. Rumour has it he is in prison, but if the authorities think this is the end of their problems, they are wrong. Somehow, the leaflets keep appearing; though how Johnny Palotski can operate a printing press from jail, nobody knows. But there is one sure-fire way of stopping him.

And so it is that one day five soldiers show up at his cell. There is a burst of gunfire and Johnny Palotski is dead before he hits the ground. But this is not enough for the army colonel. Later he goes to the mortuary to make absolutely sure they have killed the right man.

'Yes, that is Johnny Palotski,' says the colonel to the guy with the white coat, 'but I need you to do something important for me.'

He speaks quietly to the man in the white coat, who looks very surprised. And later we hear that, to make sure Johnny Palotski does not speak another word about this One Who is to Come, or any other such nonsense, they have his head cut from his body.

When the army colonel goes and reports to the regional administrator there is great relief that this trouble-maker is silenced for good. And Johnny Palotski is certainly silenced.

For five whole days there is silence. Then the leaflets start appearing again. Nobody knows where they are coming from, but somewhere, somebody is keeping alive the spirit of Johnny Palotski and bringing hope to the people who endure so much. And people even begin to think that maybe there will be someone who will come and end their suffering and that there will be life. And this makes the authorities very uneasy. For how can you silence a man who is already dead and whose head you have cut off to make sure?

Meanwhile there is a story going round that when they take Johnny's body from the prison cell, even though he is shot dead by the soldiers, there is a smile on his face. But why would anyone be smiling as they suffer such a terrible death?

Unless in those last moments Johnny Palotski is not thinking about the soldiers' guns at all, but about the one who is coming. Or maybe about Liberty Lavender.

Close to death

So this is how it will end. The stranger knows now that he is too weak to make the long trek back to the settlement that was his last contact with life. But the discovery that he will soon be dead stirs no fear or even disappointment as he continues to walk.

His face is blistered from the desert heat and his tongue too swollen with thirst to speak a word. Hour by hour the white sun is burning the moisture and life out of him.

He came to find an answer; but all he has found is death. For weeks not a living thing has been seen, except a fly that waits expectantly to lay its eggs in him.

Yesterday, it may have been yesterday, he was so hungry he dreamed he willed the stones to become bread. But then he woke and found himself still walking and forced the thought out of his mind.

Later, on a hill-top, he imagined the whole world spread out before him. And somewhere a soft voice like the buzzing of a fly was saying: 'What if all this was yours?'

Finally, in desperation, he thought of jumping to his death to force the answer he is seeking. Would he really be allowed to die?

As the last day dawns, the stranger wakes to find he is not alone. Below him in the valley a man is busy moving stones. Too weak to stand, the stranger lies where he has slept. He rests his head on his arm and watches.

The tall figure works steadily, clearing rocks and pebbles from a wide, flat area. Behind him, in the distance, another larger hill rises steeply from the desert floor. As the stranger watches, the man begins searching for large flat rocks and starts to arrange them in a long line, running across the cleared area, towards the mountain. Working quickly despite the heat, he gradually forms a long double line of rocks which, to the stranger watching from above, looks like a primitive causeway. In some powerful way the lines of rocks seem to engage with the mountain behind them, as though both have an unspoken meaning.

Finally the tall man stops. His work is finished. He stands quite still in the valley below, his back to the stranger. He is looking along the line of stones towards the mountain. For a moment he himself seems to become part of the landscape.

On the hill-top the stranger struggles slowly to his feet and sets off down to the man below, who is now standing watching his progress. But when the stranger finally reaches the valley floor, he discovers the man has disappeared.

He walks across to the start of the double row of stones which seem to point towards the mountain. Something is shining in the sun and as the stranger reaches the beginning of the stone sculpture in the desert, he finds the man has left a bottle of water.

He looks out across the valley. Through the heat haze, he can see in the distance the tall figure standing, watching him intently. The stranger tries to call out that he has left his water, but his throat is too swollen for any sound.

Finally, he opens the bottle and takes a drink. He pours a little water into his hand and splashes it over his face. He takes another drink and then another. Then he pours the rest of the water over his head; rubbing it into his short dark hair.

In the far distance the tall man stands, watching. The stranger raises the empty water bottle in thanks. The tall figure raises an arm in salutation. Then he turns and vanishes into the shimmering haze.

The stranger looks along the double row of flat stones towards the mountain which now seems much closer. He closes his eyes and kneels in the grey dust of the desert for a long time.

At last he gets to his feet. He turns and, with the mountain behind him and following the line of the stones, he begins to walk.

Somewhere ahead of him are the villages, the towns; the sea and the boats; the poor, the oppressed. And the tanks and guns of the occupying forces.

He is aware that, for the first time in forty days, the fly has disappeared. Perhaps it has gone to find other places to lay its eggs. The stranger is glad to be rid of it, though he has the feeling that, in time, it will return.

But now, in the distance, he can see the desert settlement. In his mind he can taste the food and he is smiling to himself as he remembers the cold beer they sell in these parts.

Later he raises a glass as he remembers the mysterious man who makes sculptures out of stones in a desert where there is a war going on, and where maybe nobody will ever see the things he makes – and if they do they will not understand. And the stranger thinks that, in this, the tall man is perhaps like God, who also does crazy things.

And he thinks that one of the really crazy things is that this morning he is as good as dead; and certainly the fly thinks so. But tonight, here he is having a quiet beer in a bar with music playing gently in the background.

As he sits, the waiter comes in with a tray of empty glasses and a leaflet someone has left on one of the outside tables. He puts the tray down on the bar. Lighting a cigarette, he puts on his glasses and studies the leaflet.

When he has finished reading he looks across to the stranger.

'You seen these things?' he says.

'No.'

'You are not from round here?'

'From the north.'

'Maybe you should go back there,' says the waiter. 'They write dangerous things. There will be trouble.'

'Maybe,' says the stranger thoughtfully.

A dangerous venture

There was a rumour he had been a problem child. He certainly grew up to be a real trouble-maker. And the trouble started early on.

From what I hear it was a beautiful sunny morning. Most of the fishing boats were pulled up on the lakeshore, but one was still out on the water. This is the sort of day when it feels good to be alive. The sun is hot, but not too hot. Small waves are lapping quietly on the pebbles as the stranger comes walking slowly along the shoreline.

The stranger is maybe thirty-something and wearing a pair of faded jeans and a cotton shirt. He stops when he gets opposite the boat on the lake and watches, deep in thought, as two men make a final cast of the net.

As the net splashes lightly onto the water and sinks below the surface, the big bearded one pulls out a pack of cigarettes. He offers one to the other guy but he shakes his head.

'Hey,' shouts the stranger.

'Hey what?' shouts back the bearded one in the boat.

'Come with me and I will make you fishers of men,' shouts the stranger.

'Make it fishers of women and it's a deal,' shouts the younger man in the boat.

'Maybe that too,' shouts the stranger, laughing.

'Maybe you buy the beers and we think about it,' shouts the bearded one.

'Five minutes,' calls the stranger, turning to walk up the shingle towards a bar that has white plastic chairs set out under blue umbrellas.

The cold beers are waiting on the table as the two fishermen arrive.

'So who are you?' says the bearded one, taking a good pull of beer and wiping his mouth with the back of his hand.

'Jez,' says the stranger. 'You?'

'Peter,' says the big man. 'People call me Petros.'

'The rock,' says the stranger. 'Are you a rock?'

'He has rocks in his head,' says the younger man with a grin. 'He is Petros the Rox.'

'This is my idiot brother, Andy,' says Petros the Rox. 'Always talking. One day maybe I will strangle him to shut him up and the world will be a quieter place.'

'Your boat?' asks the stranger.

'It belongs to our father.'

'You like fishing?'

'Not much; but what choice do we have?'

'I know the feeling.'

'What does your father do?'

The stranger looks pensive for a moment.

'He has interests in just about everything,' he says.

'What?'

'Carpentry. Wood.'

'Better than fish.'

'Maybe.'

An hour later the three get up from the table and walk, deep in conversation, along the shore until they reach another boat where two young men are mending the nets. They stand talking for a long time until the one called the Rox thinks maybe it is getting near time for another beer. He is about to suggest this when a very angry man suddenly appears and starts to shout at Petros and his brother, demanding to know how come there is a boat full of fish slowly going rotten back there in the sun, and why are they not taking these fish in the big baskets up to the house ready to be sold?

And the Rox, who has had just enough chilled beer to take the brakes off, tells the old guy that the fish is still in the boat because he is sick of the sight of fish and, anyway, they are planning their future. And this does not involve staying around the lakeside. So no more fishing.

At this the old man becomes even more enraged and his shouting and cursing brings a sharp-faced woman onto the scene; which would be OK, except for the fact that she is holding a fish-filleting knife.

'What is all this shouting and bad language for?' demands the sharp-faced woman who, it turns out, is the mother of the two young men who are mending their nets.

'I am shouting,' yells the old guy, 'because these two thickheads who are my sons are telling me that they are packing up fishing and going off on some crazy trip with this stranger. And who is going to do the fishing if they go?'

'If we go? There is no "if we go". We are definitely going,' says the Rox. 'We have a life to live.'

'Well,' says the woman with the knife in her hand, 'that is a very terrible thing to happen and a disgrace to your family.'

'A disgrace to my family?' yells the old man. 'It is a disaster. It will not happen.'

He turns to the two brothers and shouts wildly: 'You have a duty to stay. A duty to serve the family. The law says so. It says if a man has a rebellious son who will not obey the voice of his father . . .'

'Or his mother,' chimes in the woman with the knife.

'Or his mother,' says the old man. 'Then the father and the mother shall take hold of him and take him to the elders and say to them: "He is stubborn and rebellious and will not obey our voice. He is a drunkard." Then all the men of the city shall stone him to death. That is the law. That is why you will not go.'

The Rox takes a deep breath and says to the old man: 'This may be your law but it is not my law. We are going.'

'Well,' says the woman with the knife, 'all I can say is that I am very glad it is not my sons who are walking out on their family and bringing disgrace to those who have brought them up and to whom they have a duty to stay.'

At this the two men who have been mending the nets in the boat suddenly step forward and the older one, who it turns out is called James, says to the woman:

'Do not be upset, Mother, but me and John here have decided that we are going too.'

Suddenly there is a scream from the woman with the knife like a steam valve on a boiler has started to blow. And in a very loud voice she tells her two sons how she is not in any way upset because, in exactly five seconds from now, she is going to kill this vagrant who comes walking along the beach and is leading her boys astray. And let us see then who is going where and with whom, she says.

With this she jabs the filleting knife at the ribs of the stranger and only some quick footwork prevents him breathing his last on that very spot. Instead, Jez gives a sharp yelp as the blade punctures his nice white shirt but does no lasting damage.

It is about this point that the row is brought to an abrupt halt by an army jeep that is spotted driving slowly along the nearby coast road. The jeep stops and a young woman soldier gets out. She swings her automatic rifle over her shoulder and raises a pair of binoculars to her eyes, scanning the lakeshore.

'Time to go,' says the Rox. 'We'll see you later in the bar,' he tells Jez. 'Anyway, it's your round.'

As they sit talking of the events of the day and how family reunions are never going to be the same again, the Rox says: 'With all your talk of God and love for other people I somehow thought you would be a man of peace. But now it turns out you are a trouble-maker and no mistake. But I suppose this makes the whole deal more interesting,' he adds.

'I didn't come to bring peace,' says Jez. 'I've come to set a son against his father, a daughter against her mother.'

'The younger generation against the older,' says the Rox.

'I warn you,' says Jez, 'to come with me you need to take up your cross. He who finds his life will lose it, but he who loses his life for my sake will find it.'

The four are greatly alarmed by the mention of death, since there have been many recent executions by the army of occupation and a lot of other people have disappeared into the military holding camps in the desert that have razor-wire fences and out of which nobody ever returns.

And maybe catching fish on a lake does not sound so bad after all and there is some debate as to whether this adventure is really such a good idea, when the Rox suddenly stands up:

'I'm coming with you,' he tells Jez. 'Whether these guys come or not. You are the Boss.'

Then Andy says he cannot let the big man go on his own, and so he will come along too. Just to keep an eye on his brother. The two others also decide to risk it, though this may be to do with the thought of what the fierce lady with the knife might do to them if they go back home.

'Well,' Jez says to Petros. 'Maybe you are the rock after all. In the morning we set out.'

'But first we have another beer,' says the Rox.

A rude awakening

At first nobody can work out why the Rox is so bad-tempered these days. Especially in the mornings, when it is not wise to speak to him. Then, slowly, we begin to figure it out. The Rox may be big but he is not without feelings. And one of the things he is sensitive about is a lack of sleep.

The problem is that the boys have been on the road for days and it seems that the Rox is a bit old for the outdoor life, especially when it is cold and raining. But the Boss says that from now on things should be getting better as we are heading for a town which he knows. In fact he was brought up there. And he is certain they will find warm and comfortable beds; and maybe even cooked breakfasts.

The Rox is very happy about this, especially the thought of cooked breakfasts, and says how much he enjoys the gentle hum of urban life. So, after we arrive and have supper, he announces he will get himself an early night. And off the big man goes to bed.

Very soon he is sleeping soundly and all is well with the world. Until a little after three in the morning, that is, when there is an explosion of noise so deafening that the Rox leaps right out of his bed holding his ears to stop the pain. The din is louder than anything he has heard in his life as rock music blasts across the town.

The others are also wide awake and holding their heads with the pain the noise is causing. They cannot speak to each other because no one can hear what is being said.

This hell on earth goes on for twenty or thirty minutes and then, without any warning, suddenly stops. But the Boss and the Rox and the others will not take their hands away from their ears in case the deafening noise starts up again; and so they do not hear the woman who runs the place where they are staying, even though she is knocking urgently on the door.

She finally makes herself heard and is very apologetic for not warning them of the noise, which she says is happening several nights a week. The Rox, who is a sensitive person and is extremely unhappy with all these goings on, says some very rude words and asks just who in hell is making such a noise in the middle of the night.

And the woman says it is the occupation forces who have this army truck with loudspeakers the size of refrigerators on the back who drive round in the middle of the night to shake up the residents and remind them who is in charge.

Meanwhile, across the street, there is the sound of children screaming from the fear and the woman says all this is having a very bad effect, especially on the younger ones who are afraid to go to sleep and are wetting the bed and generally going crazy from the noise and not knowing whether the soldiers will come and take away their parents. And the parents feel humiliated on account of not being able to protect their children from this suffering.

Many people are going mad from the way they are treated, while others just want to pack up and leave. Except there is nowhere to go, as the occupation forces have put a concrete barrier round the town so no one can escape. And so they are trapped like animals in a cage.

But things go from bad to the other thing the next morning when the Boss decides to go to the Meeting Place where the Robed Ones hold the weekly prayers. Normally prayers are a pretty quiet activity, although there have been times when the Boss has got himself into trouble for breaking the rules somewhat.

But this morning he just walks in and sits down with the local people, many of whom recognize him from the time when he is growing up in the town, and there is a general buzz of welcome around the place.

So welcoming are they, that the Boss is invited to read from the Holy Book – which is a great honour. So he stands up and finds the place in the writings of some big cheese called Isaiah, or some-such, and reads:

The Spirit of the Lord is upon me,
because he has anointed me to preach good news to the poor.
He has sent me to proclaim release to the captives
and recovery of sight to the blind,
to set at liberty those who are oppressed,
to proclaim the acceptable year of the Lord.

Then he closes the book and hands it back to the attendant and sits down. And everything is quiet and peaceful. But only for a minute.

'Today,' says the Boss, 'this writing has come true. In your hearing.'

At this a general discussion starts up with some people saying how well he speaks, for a local boy. But others, the more they think about it, are not so happy because he seems to be saying that he is like the big cheese who wrote the holy words – that he also is chosen by God in a special way which has not happened for many long years.

Meanwhile, other people are getting pretty anxious at all this talk of liberty for those who are oppressed and good news for the poor and freedom for those who are held captive. Because they know they are the ones held captive by a powerful foreign army of occupation and they are oppressed by the noise machines that come in the night and tear their lives apart until they think they will go mad.

But, most of all, they know what happens to uppity people who start talking about freedom: their homes get bulldozed into rubble and they disappear into military detention camps – or into the prisons run by their own leaders who collude with the Army. They end up dead.

And suddenly panic grips them and they want the Boss thrown out there and then before any of this dangerous talk gets back to the authorities: to the Army and to the Robed Ones whose preaching about the religious laws sometimes seems as deafening as the noise machines that come in the night.

And what has been a quiet prayer meeting suddenly erupts in a general riot with some guy yelling that he is going to get a gun and, for a while, it looks like this might be the end of everything. And a fine welcome home this is turning out to be.

The gang only just make it out of the town, thanks largely to the Rox who pushes and shoves and makes a way through the crowd so the gang can get away. And afterwards everybody is pretty shaken up.

Later in the day, when things have calmed down a touch, Andy is talking to the Boss and asks him why he chooses that bit of the holy writings, especially as it almost costs him his life.

But the Boss seems to be saying that this does not happen by accident. From what Andy tells us later it seems like these words about good news for the poor and freedom for the captives are the guts of what the Boss is doing.

But Andy says that, if this is so, there is going to be more trouble in the pipeline; for this guy Isaiah writes some very disturbing things. And he tells the Boss that maybe he should choose a different bit of the holy writings to hang his hat on; unless he believes this good news to the poor stuff is a matter of life and death. But the Boss seems to think it really is a matter of life and death – and probably both.

And it seems to me a tragic thing when people are too oppressed to even hear the word of freedom when it is spoken to them. But perhaps that is what captivity means: when people's minds have been taken over and controlled so they can no longer think for themselves or hear the still small voice of God.

Which is maybe worse than being dead.

Giving it all you've got

I have to admit that in the great hierarchy of birds, we sparrows are not well placed. On the top perch are birds like the eagle and the swan. Lower down the pecking order, as you might say, are performance artists like the woodpecker, kingfisher and cormorant. And down at the bottom of the heap are the trash: starlings, pigeons and sparrows. Even the Boss admits it.

'Sparrows? Two a penny,' he says.

For a moment, I am quite shocked. But you never quite know what the Boss is up to. He comes out with ordinary comments that pass you by – but then they come round and hit you on the back of the head. Suddenly I get to thinking he is saying sparrows may be two a penny, but even they are valued by God.

In the crazy upside down way the Boss talks, you never know who is at the bottom and who is at the top. Most of his friends are sparrows – the human variety, I mean. The poor, the hungry, the ignored, the overlooked. Yet there are times when these sparrow people seem more important than anyone else to him. People who get pushed to the margins are somehow at the centre in his way of thinking. And one day something happens that proves it.

Jez and the gang, who are now numbering maybe eight or ten guys, are taking the breeze in the old part of the city. As they are hanging around, the Boss sees something going on outside the big religion place: the Citadel or whatever they call it. Technicians are buzzing about in a state of great agitation. An advertising hoarding has been erected and TV cameras are being set up.

From what I can see it looks like the launch of some sort of campaign. The Robed Ones are there, of course: this is their patch. And many rich people, dressed up like they're off to the races, are beginning to congregate and to jostle for a position where the TV cameras will see them.

Suddenly into the Citadel courtyard glides a big stretch-limo which pulls up right in front of the cameras. Out of it climb two serious-looking guys in dark suits with sunglasses and little earphones – and bulges in their jackets that make you think you might not argue with them after all.

One of them opens the boot of the limo and out comes a big sheet of cardboard which turns out to be one of those giant cheques that are so big that everyone watching TV will be able to see how much the cheque is for. And who it is from.

And right now Who It Is From is getting out of the white limo and we see it is none other than the big business tycoon Mr Sly Mammon and his good wife; though no one is entirely sure how good she is or, come to think about it, whether or not she is his wife.

But Mr Mammon runs some trans-global enterprise making millions by the day, and so he does not mind about that. It is enough for him that she is a very attractive young woman who likes expensive clothes and sun tans and skirts that stop well short of her knees. And a little hat that, when I look closer, seems to be made out of bits of some relative of mine.

Suddenly two soldiers come marching up. They have shiny brass bugles on red, white and blue coloured cords and they start to belt out a fanfare which tells one and all that something important is about to happen, and that ordinary people should shut up and pay great attention.

Then one of the Robed Ones steps up to the microphone and his voice comes booming out across the courtyard like someone announcing a heavyweight boxing match.

'Ladies and gentlemen,' he bellows. 'We are honoured to welcome one of the nation's leading businessmen, Mr Sly Mammon, who has come here to present us with a wonderful donation to launch our Citadel fundraising appeal.'

He goes on in this manner for some time with Mr Mammon grinning at the TV cameras and showing off the diamond he has had set in one of his teeth so it glitters in the sun in a way which seems very attractive to people. Especially those who have nothing.

Finally the cheque is handed over and when the amount is revealed there is great amazement, even among the rich and beautiful ones, for the cheque is for a cool half million. Which is very strange because Mr Mammon is not known to part willingly with even a penny.

But now the generous Mr Mammon is making a very modest speech sounding like he is Mother Teresa. As he is talking I can see a fly that has been buzzing around has landed on his shoulder, though he does not seem to mind this.

As soon as Mr Mammon is through talking, the Robed One bounces back to the microphone and yells out: 'Half a million! What a wonderful start to our appeal.'

Then the lesser mortals begin to come up and hand over their cheques and each time the Robed One yells out the amount. One hundred thousand! Fifty thousand! Twenty thousand!

Suddenly there is a small commotion at the edge of the crowd where it seems the security guards are having trouble with some old lady who is trying to get through. After a struggle, she manages to get past the bodyguards. She walks slightly unsteadily towards the guy at the microphone and puts something in his hand.

For a moment he looks taken aback; but this boy knows how to work a crowd. 'Two brass farthings!' he yells in just the same amazed voice that he has announced the big donations from the rich and beautiful people.

And the crowd howl with laughter at the old woman who has gate-crashed this prestigious event. The laughter carries on as she walks slowly away. But as I look down from the ledge where I am perched I notice the Boss isn't laughing. Though there is an odd smile on his face.

When the laughter has died down he calls to the gang, who are still studying Mrs Mammon's sun tan: 'See that old girl who just handed over her money? How much was it?'

'Two farthings,' says the Rox.

'Well,' says the Boss, 'I'm telling you that woman has given more than all the other people here put together.'

There is a confused silence as the gang try to unravel this mystery.

'She has given the last of her money to God,' he says. 'She has nothing left in the world. The rest gave out of their riches – and they have plenty left.'

And suddenly it feels like one of those sparrow moments when everything is turned upside down and the least are more important than the top people.

'Come on,' says the Boss, 'we've got to go see a friend.'

'Who's that?' says the Rox.

'Someone who's going to bed hungry tonight unless we can find her some food.'

On the way the guys are talking about the limo and Mrs Mammon's tan and Andy says: 'That big cheque they were waving around was a complete load of rubbish. Did you know that Mammon's got the contract for the building work on the Citadel? He'll make his half-million back in no time.'

And the Rox suddenly says: 'Did you notice that fly that settled on Mammon's shoulder just as he was making his speech?'

The Boss says yes he did notice. He has a faraway look in his eye and, for a moment, he suddenly looks very sad, like the sun has gone in. Later I remember that look. But by then it is too late.

Two angry women

He could very well have been the first man in history to die in such a way. And in truth it would not have looked good on the headstone for people to read: 'Killed by a dinner plate.'

But that is how it nearly ended for the Boss, who in one day manages to get the wrong side of two very angry ladies. And then where would we all have been?

The day starts out well, as I remember. The best of all possible days. A big meal is on offer and there are few things the guys like better than getting their faces round food, specially the way Betty cooks. Betty is actually not the name on her driving licence, which shows her to have the very old-fashioned name of Martha. But Martha hates this name which she says reminds her of boiled cabbage, and in no way will she answer to such a title. And in this she is very convincing, not least because Martha is a very strong-minded person with whom you do not argue.

Which is how the Boss almost meets his end.

He and the gang have been asked round to the home of Betty and her sister for grub. And for growing boys with an itinerant lifestyle, this is very good news. Especially as Betty is an inspired woman in the kitchen.

So at four in the afternoon when the sun is just beginning to ease up, they all arrive at the house, even though this is a good hour before the eating is due to begin. Out back there is the sound of pans and general commotion and Betty emerges, red in the face from all the cooking that is going on.

The guys naturally give her a big wave and say how delighted they are to be there for the feed. And Betty is feeling pretty good too, since there are few things more pleasing to her than boys who like their food – especially when she is the cook. Not only that, she is very fond of the Boss and is very happy that he has come to her home, which will be a big thing among the neighbours for many days to come.

Meanwhile her sister, who is not at all like Betty, being somewhat shy and quiet, is setting out the knives and forks and putting several bottles of wine on the table. Pretty soon the job is done, but instead of going back into the steam room where Betty is having a busy old time, the quiet one, who is called Mary, slips out onto the sidewalk where the Boss is talking to the boys and some other people who have drifted by.

And in no time at all she and the others are deeply engrossed in what the Boss has to say about the love of God and how it is built on justice and respect for all people and how there can be no peace without this justice which means all people are of equal worth.

Now it is just as he is saying the word 'peace' that all hell suddenly breaks loose. Betty, who has emerged from the house, is standing there snorting like a bull and telling her little sister that a woman's place is in the kitchen and how can she do all the work on her own? In short, that she should get off her backside and come and help with the cooking. Right now.

The boys are in general agreement with this, since they feel it is natural that a woman's place is in the kitchen and not sitting with the men debating matters of significance. And in any case they do not want to jeopardize the big feed which is coming their way. So Mary gets up to follow Betty into the kitchen where great clouds of steam are now issuing. And it is then that the Boss makes his first mistake.

'Hold on there, Bets,' he says in a very friendly manner. 'Mary is doing no harm sitting out here, since it is good for all people, men and women, to listen to new things.'

In fact, says the Boss, she is choosing the better thing by doing so, for I am not always going to be around. So be at peace, he tells her.

But his words do not incline Betty to be peaceful, and she starts shouting and yelling even more and dashes back into the kitchen.

Now the Boss, who normally understands human nature, follows in order to speak further to his friend. But what he doesn't realize is that she has gone back to grab a rolling pin. Or maybe a meat skewer.

Fortunately when she gets back into the kitchen she cannot immediately lay her hands on the rolling pin or a meat skewer and, instead, picks up a twelve-inch dinner plate and heaves it at the Boss like an athlete hurling a discus. But her hands are still wet from the cooking so the plate goes slightly off course, hitting the door-post not half an inch from the Boss's head. He ducks out of the way, but he is far too slow and if her hands had not been wet the plate would have ended his days there and then. And maybe ruined a good meal too.

Instead they stand there staring at each other, both pretty shook up at what might have happened. Suddenly, there is a commotion outside; which is maybe a good thing, as Betty has just remembered where she keeps the meat skewers.

The kitchen door bursts open and the Rox comes charging in yelling that the Boss must come quickly. Some woman has been caught breaking the law and is going to be stoned to death – an ancient custom, and not the most agreeable spectacle right before a meal.

The Boss and Betty, who seems to have forgotten about the argument, at least for the moment, belt through to the front of the house and into the street. There they find a woman being slapped around by a crowd of angry men: among whom are a number of Robed Ones.

'Hey,' says a large man in black robes when he sees the Boss. 'What do we do with this woman we have here? She was caught in the act of adultery – with a man who is not her husband. The law says she should be put to death by stoning. What do you say, wise one?'

And as he says this, he shoves the woman so hard she falls flat down in the dust and everybody can see her clothes are all ripped and her face is coming up with big bruises and it looks like someone has bust her nose for there is blood all over the place. Even so she is shouting and raging, though nobody can catch what she is saying.

The Boss squats down in front of the woman and writes something slowly in the dust. The Rox is looking over the Boss's shoulder and sees what he is writing. The Rox is not so good at reading; but, even so, he should be able to manage this, for it is in block capitals.

'What's it say?' Andy asks him.

'Dunno,' says the Rox. 'It's foreign. Says: TEIUQ EB.'

For a moment Andy is silent, then gives the Rox a shove.

'You big fandango. He's writing upside down for her to read. He's telling her to Be Quiet.'

By now the Boss is standing up and he says very deliberately to the Robed Ones: 'OK. Go ahead. Stone her.'

There is a murmur from the crowd. Then he adds: 'But the one among you who is perfect has to throw the first brick.'

Then he squats down in the dust with the woman again, so that if anyone starts throwing rocks they are going to hit him as well. But no one throws anything and, instead, the crowd slowly start to edge away until finally there is no one left.

The Boss helps the woman to her feet.

'Does no one condemn you?' he says.

'No,' she answers. But her voice sounds a bit strange.

'Neither do I,' says Jez. 'Go on your way. And do not sin again.'

At this, a very amazing thing happens for, instead of thanking him, the woman suddenly starts shouting at him and beating on his chest with her fists and finally walks off, kicking up the dust with her feet. Then she turns and makes a gesture that leaves no one in any doubt as to her feelings.

All of which leaves the Boss somewhat confused. But, hey, suddenly the food is ready and this time the plates stay on the table and the boys get stuck in to a big Betty Special with extra chips on the side. And the problems of the day are forgotten.

But down the street I spot the woman with the bust nose hanging around. Which is something I do not understand; although one day it will all be made clear. But the Boss may find he is still not completely out of trouble.

Up the money tree

These days the Boss is getting to be big news just about wherever he goes, what with the battles he has with the Robed Ones and the care and respect he always shows the drop-outs and homeless people he meets.

It is like the map of the world has been turned upside down and the poor and outcast at the bottom are suddenly at the top. But the rich and successful people are out in the cold.

'They have had their reward already,' the Boss once said.

Not that he wasn't for giving people a second chance. Like the rich guy up the tree. That was a strange event, which happened roughly as follows.

One day the gang comes to this town in the middle of who knows where. But word has got around, and such a big crowd turns out that the Boss can hardly walk down the street. The Rox is in front pushing a way through like a bulldozer, but the rest are lost in the crowd.

Being a sparrow is a fine thing: you can always see what's going on. And right now I can see a fat little guy jumping up and down and getting very cross with the crowd.

He is trying to see the Boss, but he is too small and the crowd are not letting him through to the front. In fact, the way I read the situation, they dislike this little guy greatly for some reason; and they are making sure he knows it.

Personally, I do not have any animosity towards people who are small and stocky; particularly as I myself have occasionally been referred to in those terms. Anyway, this guy may be small and fat, but he is also smart, for suddenly he scoots off down the street till he comes to a big tree. And up he goes.

His expensive clothes get somewhat torn in the process and his shiny black shoes are badly scuffed, but in a couple of minutes he is out on a branch overhanging the road – clinging on for dear life. As the crowd pass underneath, the Boss looks up at the little man on the branch and bursts out laughing.

'Hey, Zakko,' he says, 'come down out of the tree: I need to talk to you.'

But Zak cannot climb backwards along the branch; which is a very difficult thing to do, even for a cat. Which he is definitely not. At first the crowd are cheering as he struggles to get back along the branch, but suddenly they start shouting and swearing when they realize who it is up the tree. And everyone seems greatly pleased when this Mr Zak finally falls out of the tree and lands very heavily in the road, right where the Boss is standing.

There is some disappointment that Mr Zak has not broken his neck, though he is wobbling plenty on account of hitting the ground so hard. Many people are saying they would like to lynch Mr Zak, who it turns out is a big crook, and has caused many people great pain. But the Boss has other ideas:

'Zak,' he says, 'I must come and have dinner with you today.'

Now this is a highly unpopular announcement as far as the crowd are concerned, since having a meal with someone is a clear sign of friendship. Meanwhile, it is well known that Zak is not just a crook but also a traitor because he collects the tax money for the army of occupation, as well as the Citadel taxes levied by the Robed Ones. On top of that there is also the local tax money the people have to pay. And, after all that, the greedy Mr Zak then scoops up a large dollop of extra cash for himself.

Four times over he takes money from the poor and leaves them so deep in debt that they are half starving and have to sell their homes and any bits of land they may have for growing things on. Many of them become destitute and have to beg on the streets and become the people the newspapers, who are owned by rich people, call parasites and scroungers.

And the Boss is going to go eat with this grasping crook?

The gang, who have now managed to catch up with the Boss, are also uneasy about this announcement, especially the Rox. But Mr Zak is as pleased as a dog with two tails and hobbles off down the road to make the preparations for the meal.

So there we all are, two hours later, sitting on the terrace of Mr Zak's fine house overlooking his large swimming pool. Meanwhile the crowd, who have managed to get through the big iron security fence, are standing on his lawn and on the flower beds. But Mr Zak doesn't seem to mind this at all. Instead he taps a spoon on his glass and stands up to make a speech, and I can see he has a funny look on his face.

'If I have robbed anybody . . .' he starts off.

'Robbed anybody? You've robbed everybody,' yells a voice from the crowd. 'You sucked their blood and left them to die.'

Andy turns to the Boss: 'Let's get out of here.'

And maybe he is right, for the crowd are out for revenge on this crook and some people are even yelling that they should burn down the very nice home Mr Zak has bought himself with their money.

But the Boss is watching Mr Zak, who is holding up his hand. And now the crowd goes quiet for it seems that Mr Zak is very distressed and tears are running down his plump cheeks.

'If I have robbed anyone I will pay them back,' he says. There is a murmur of approval. 'I will pay them back not just what I stole, I will restore it four times over.'

There is cheering from the people standing on the lawn and in the flower beds but the fat guy is still not finished: 'And half of all that I own I will give to the poor.'

And the Boss says to Zak: 'Life has come to this house today.'

At last the cheering and yelling finally dies down, but the Rox does not seem very happy with what has happened.

'So is that it?' he says. 'Is he forgiven all the suffering he's caused? He's bought his way out of trouble, that's all.'

'Don't we want our debts to be forgiven?' says the Boss.

'But how far does that go?' says the Rox doggedly, still not willing to let it pass. 'If someone keeps on wronging me, do I have to keep on forgiving them? And how many times do I have to do that? Four times? Five times? Seven times?'

'No, Rox,' says the Boss. 'Not seven times. Seventy times seven.'

Suddenly they realize that, while they have been arguing, a party has started and people are dancing on the lawn and in the flower beds; while others have jumped into the swimming pool, even though they still have their clothes on.

'Oh well,' says the Rox, his anger subsiding. 'Where's the little fat guy? I need a drink.'

Love your enemy

There is nothing like a public hanging to cheer people up. Today's general mood of despondency has been lifted by the news that two soldiers have been captured by the rebels. As soon as someone can find a rope they are to be strung up in the area of wrecked buildings that yesterday was the village square.

Before the tanks came it was a nice little place. Not posh with fountains, but a place the Boss liked to come to drink coffee and talk to the people about this and that; about God and freedom.

But now the tanks have destroyed many of the shops and houses in the centre of the village and heavy gunfire has smashed up the other buildings so badly that few are inhabitable.

A snatch squad of soldiers had followed the tanks in the night raid in the hope of capturing some of the rebels. But word of the attack had got out, and not only did they leave empty-handed, but two young conscripts who became separated from the main force were captured.

In the dawn silence the two soldiers now stand in the rubble they have helped to create, waiting for death. The Boss and the others join the crowd that begins to gather.

As I watch from the top of a half-demolished wall, the two prisoners are standing in the middle of a circle of armed rebels. The Boss and the rest of the gang have pushed through to the front of the crowd so that they are only a few feet away from the ring of rebel fighters. Most have rifles but others have got themselves rocket launchers which they carry as a badge of courage as much as a serious threat to the Army.

One of the rebel leaders is talking to the two prisoners whose guns and other gear are thrown down in the dust. People in the growing crowd are yelling for the soldiers to be hanged. A woman's home has been demolished by the tanks and she is screaming and seems like she is going to fall down in a faint.

The morning sun makes dark shadows across the night's devastation and as the air gets warmer, the anger of the crowd is also heating up.

'We need to get the hell out of here. They're going to shoot them,' mutters the Rox as he watches the circle of armed men surrounding the prisoners.

'I don't think so,' replies the Boss.

'You're right,' says Andy. 'If they open fire on the prisoners now, they'll kill their own people on the other side of the circle. The circle's their guarantee of safety. For the moment.'

The rebel spokesman is now shouting something at one of the young soldiers. Suddenly he grabs the young prisoner's wrist and, pulling him towards him, he forces his hand against his chest.

'What do you feel there?' he shouts.

'Your heart,' answers the soldier sullenly.

'My heart,' says the rebel. 'I have a heart – like you have a heart. I have kids. I have a wife. I have a family. All I want is to live. All I want is freedom. You know what is going to happen to you?'

The young soldier mumbles words no one can hear.

'What do you say?' shouts the rebel.

'You are going to kill us,' says the soldier, now with a hint of defiance in his voice.

'Kill you?' shouts the rebel. 'No. We do not do that. You too have a heart. You too maybe have children. You too maybe have a wife. You too want to live. Why should we kill you?'

He turns and shouts something into the crowd and a moment later a man appears with an old metal tray and small cups of the thick black coffee they drink round here.

'You drink,' says the man. 'I am sorry for the dust on the cups. We have not had a good night.'

'Are you going to let us go?' says the young conscript.

'Let you go? No. We will not let you go. You might get lost. You might get hurt. I will tell you what happens: you tell your commanding officer to come here himself and fetch you. He will look after you. If he has courage to walk in here, you all go safely. Why should we want to harm you?'

'He will not come,' says the young soldier. 'Why do you want him to come here?'

'Why do I want him to come here?' asks the rebel. Suddenly he puts his hand against his own chest. 'So he can see I have a heart. That I am a human being too. Maybe he will have some coffee – though today it is not so good, the coffee, with the bad night we have had.'

As they drink there is a moment's silence and then a shout from the back of the crowd. One dreaded word: helicopters. Suddenly everyone can hear the distant chatter of the blades as the black helicopters approach, sweeping in from the south to try to locate the missing men. Or maybe simply to pound the area with rockets.

'You maybe talk to them?' says the rebel leader.

But the soldier is already on his knees desperately trying to get his radio to work.

'Hear me. Hear me,' he yells into the handset. 'Do not attack. Repeat. Do not attack. Do you read me? Do you read me? Do not attack. We are safe.'

The four military helicopters are now closing in and the sound of the engines is deafening. I am almost blown off the wall by the downdraught from their rotors. They hover for a few moments as though unsure of what to do. Then they move off into the distance – but ready to return at any moment.

The crowd are silent as they wait to see what will happen next.

More shouting on the radio follows. More coffee appears. Finally a jeep shows up on the outskirts of the village and stops. A lone uniformed figure gets out and starts walking through the rubble that is in the road from the demolished buildings. He keeps coming on towards the crowd.

The rebel leader watches him for some time and then turns to the young soldier: 'He is a brave man. Maybe he too has a heart.'

So we do not get a lynching after all; but nobody has been bored with the morning's events.

Later the Boss is hanging out with the gang and some of the people with the guns and the guy who talks to the prisoners is there as well. Andy is saying they should have killed the two soldiers and how it should be that one soldier is killed for every villager the Army kills: an eye for an eye.

But the Boss does not buy this. And he turns to the gang and the others who are hanging around the place and says: 'Love your enemies. Pray for those who curse you. Do good to those who hate you. Pray for those who treat you badly.'

There is a dead silence after that, which means people are not sure they like what they have heard. And he grins and says it again, just so there is no mistake: 'Love your enemies.'

It is a few days later that we hear there is trouble at the army compound because, when they get back, the two prisoners refuse to go out on any more patrols. And many of the other soldiers also say that they are not going to smash up any more villages because they reckon the people there are people like them.

But others say it is because they are scared to get captured in case they are made to drink the coffee.

Half a loaf

Maybe it was because they never had any money and often did not know where their next meal was coming from, but the gang were always interested in food. And it was often when they were eating that some of the strangest things happened.

Sometimes it was big meals where they'd been invited as somebody's guest: but the oddest thing came about because of a simple loaf of bread. And it wasn't freshly baked, I can tell you. It happened one day in the late spring. The rains had stopped and the grass had not yet been burned off by the sun.

As the gang wake up they find the Boss has gone off on his own, as he often does, to have some time to think and be quiet. But this time he does not come back as normal, and so eventually the gang set out to look for him. Word is that he has been seen heading up the valley towards the hills. As they walk they realize other people are also making their way along the winding road through the valley.

Finally they find him out on a hillside. But he isn't getting much in the way of peace. A small crowd has already begun to gather and more people are arriving by the minute. By noon there are a couple of thousand people; maybe more. And that is worrying, for the Army have imposed a law forbidding large crowds and demonstrations to try to stop the rebels staging another uprising. The result is that people are uneasy in case an army patrol should suddenly appear and they all end up in jail.

It is a fine day and so far there has been no sign of the Army, though a couple of the Robed Ones are hanging around at the back. Meanwhile the Boss is talking to the crowd about what he calls the Kingdom and how they are all valued by God – regardless of who they are.

But that message isn't going down too well with some of the crowd, who seem intent on ejecting a rough-looking youth. He has been trying to beg money off people in the crowd, but they aren't having any of it. Whether or not God values him, they don't seem to.

It is late in the afternoon when the crisis develops; and it centres on the Rox's stomach. He is getting hungry, and he is not one to suffer in silence. Not only is he hungry: other people are also getting hungry. And it is a long way to the shops.

Suddenly someone at the back of the crowd calls out: 'Hey, We need some food. What about food?'

The Rox turns to the Boss: 'We need some food.'

'So?' says Jez. 'Do something about it.'

The Rox shouts out to the people in the crowd: 'Who's got some food?'

There is silence.

He shouts again: 'Come on, who's got some food: we need to eat.'

'They have no food,' shouts the voice at the back of the crowd.

'OK,' says the Rox, turning to the Boss. 'Now what?'

'Get them to sit down. But ask them to sit in groups: groups of ten or fifteen.'

'You're joking,' says the Rox. 'What use will that be?'

Then he catches the look in the Boss's eye and goes off to try to get the crowd to divide up into groups. But he is still not happy.

Meanwhile the youth who has been ejected from the crowd has made his way to the front and is talking to Andy and James.

They walk over to the Boss: 'He's got a loaf of bread: well, what's left of a loaf. He says we can have it if we want it.'

The Boss comes over and speaks to the lad. The boy's arms are bruised and ulcerated and there are open sores on his face and neck.

'Heroin?' he says.

The boy is silent.

'How old are you?'

'Eighteen.'

'Eighteen?'

'Sixteen.'

'What's your name?'

'Matthew.'

The Boss takes the bread from the boy.

'I won't forget this.'

When the Rox has got the crowd sitting in groups, the Boss holds up the loaf of bread. 'We have food,' he calls out.

A few people in the crowd laugh when they see the half-eaten loaf the Boss is holding up. Then he breaks the bread in pieces and gives it to the gang:

'Hand it out.'

They look at him as though he is mad.

'There are a couple of thousand people here,' says the Rox urgently, 'and they are hungry. Are you kidding?'

'Hand it out,' says the Boss.

Reluctantly they each take a piece of bread and set off across the grass to the different groups. There is going to be trouble. Andy gets to the first group and offers them the bread.

There is a moment of embarrassed silence; then one of the men says: 'Actually, I've got some food of my own.'

As the people in the group realize they all have food with them, they begin to share what they have brought.

Gradually others start to do the same. People begin to laugh and talk until the whole hillside is like a huge party.

Finally, when everyone has finished eating, the Boss stands up and calls for silence. He turns to the young boy who gave the loaf of bread.

'We need to say thank you to this young man,' he says to the crowd. 'He shared his dinner with us.'

There is a roar of applause.

The Boss holds up his hand for quiet.

'Remember this. It's important. Give and it will be given to you. The generosity you show to others will be the measure of what you receive.'

The young lad looks at the Boss: 'That was a miracle,' he says with admiration.

'You made it happen,' says the Boss.

The Rox, however, is confused and still slightly annoyed at having to try to organize the large crowd.

'So why did they have to sit in small groups?' he says.

'So they could see each other?' says Andy, cutting in. 'Face to face, as people. None of them wanted to admit they had food with them in case no one else had. Not until we started handing out Matthew's bread. They were all afraid of losing what they'd got. Like the rich are scared of losing what they've got. Right?' he says, suddenly turning to the Boss.

There is a smile on Jez's face.

'What now?' says the Rox.

'Collect up the left-overs and take them back to town,' says the Boss. 'Matthew's probably got friends who could do with some supper. And we need to find him some clean needles.'

The last laugh

Seems to me it's time sparrows were included under the Child Protection laws. Watching the gang, it's like some of these guys have never grown up. But for sparrows, life is different. Most people think we are just cute little things hopping around having a good time. But, from the cracking of the egg, things are tough for sparrows.

The first thing you realize is what a dangerous place you've been born into. Home is twenty feet up a tree or maybe a bundle of twigs tucked under the eaves of some guy's house. The second thing you discover is that there aren't any stairs. So, how are you going to get down to where the worms live and where there are other bits of food lying around? No one tells you how it's done. But, one morning, you suddenly find you are perched on the edge of this bundle of twigs called home, being urged to leap to certain death. The gang keep going on about the leap of faith: they do not know the meaning of the word.

Suddenly there is a shove from someone behind you, and before you know what day it is, you are plummeting towards the ground. Hopefully you remember you have wings. Somehow you manage to hit the ground feet-first. You are alive: but apart from next door's cat, you are on your own.

Not so with the human race: and the gang in particular. Even when we are on the road someone or other is always calling home. Personally, I do not care who is phoning whom. Except that one day these phone calls cause a big bust-up: like the gang is coming apart at the seams.

The trouble is the Boss. Jez is sometimes portrayed as being the patron saint of happy families, but I have to tell you this is baloney.

Not only is he very doubtful about families, he is even known to speak somewhat harshly to his own mother and brothers.

Like the day they show up when the Boss is talking to a big crush of people in someone's house. So big is the squeeze that they cannot get in, and so word is passed along that his mother and brothers are outside and are very concerned about him.

They are worried he is going too far with this talk of love for the poor. And they are afraid he is getting himself into trouble with the authorities. They even think he may not be so good in the head; for who believes in a God who gives two monkeys for the poor anyway?

Meanwhile, someone in the house gets word to the Boss, saying: 'Your mother and brothers are outside. They are very worried about you. Sounds like they want you to come home.'

But the Boss is not in any mood to break off what he is doing and meet up with his nearest and dearest, and so he replies:

'My mother and my brothers? Who are my mother and my brothers?'

And he looks round at the crowd of general riff-raff sitting with him and says: 'These are my mother and my brothers: the ones who do the will of my Father in heaven.'

When these comments are relayed to his mother and brothers outside they are very upset. Later, as she is walking home, his mother realizes her little boy really has flown the nest and has become his own person.

And it is a strange thing but, after a while, she starts showing up at the places where the Boss is talking; like she is one of the crowd. Maybe a friend. And that seems OK with him.

But what is not OK is when the mother of two of the gang shows up and starts shouting the odds. Her sons have been complaining they are not getting the recognition they deserve. They want to be the leaders of the gang: second in command to the Boss.

Now the rest of the gang are appalled at this. Being a leader is not what the deal is about, and the Boss is often saying that he is here to serve and not to be served, and such-like.

But this thought has clearly been omitted from the phone calls home, for one morning a very large lady appears on the scene, demanding that changes are made.

'Give orders that in your kingdom these two boys of mine may sit next to you, one at your right hand and the other at your left,' says this big Esmeralda in a voice which does not give the least hint of compromise.

The Boss sits with his head in his hands for some minutes and I am sure I hear him saying some words under his breath; though I cannot swear what those words may have been.

Then he glances up at big Esmeralda who looks like she could go all the way in a world wrestling contest.

'To sit at my right hand or at my left is not mine to grant,' he says.

This to-ing and fro-ing goes on for some time until, realizing she is not making any headway with the Boss, big Esmeralda gives a snort and leaves; scattering men, women and chairs in her wake.

As peace returns, the Boss turns to the gang and, with a somewhat weary voice, tells them yet again how they have got hold of the stick at the wrong end:

'You know how it is in the world: the rulers lord it over their subjects and the great make their authority felt. But with you it is different. Among you whoever wants to be great must be your servant and whoever wants to be first must be the slave of all.

'Remember what I told you: the first shall be last and the last shall be first.'

But, as often happens, the Rox seems unwilling to let the matter rest.

'So who is this "last" who is going to be first?' he says.

And the Boss starts to explain in words even the Rox will understand that the 'last' is maybe a figure of speech.

The conversation is getting somewhat gritty, but the debate comes to a sudden halt when the door opens and in walks a lady. Except the Rox does not think that this is any lady – for it is none other than the woman who the crowd are planning to stone to death a few weeks back.

'Who let that slapper in here?' shouts the Rox, who is pretty fired up from his argument with the Boss. And even Andy is heard to comment that she is indeed the last person they expect to come walking in through the door.

Suddenly things go very quiet as everybody realizes that an adulteress with a busted nose is exactly that: the last person anyone expects to come breezing in.

And the Rox turns to Jez and says: 'So? The last shall be first? Someone like her is going to be first? You have got to be joking.'

But, from the look on the Boss's face, he is not joking.

Neither is the young woman with the busted nose, for she is walking purposefully across the room and keeps on walking till she is standing right up against the Rox. Then she grabs hold of the front of his trousers and smiles. And, by the distress on the face of the Rox, she has a strong grip.

'You should be more careful how you speak to people,' she says, very quietly. 'Try to learn a little respect, perhaps.'

And the Rox gives a yelp of pain as if some extra pressure has suddenly been exerted.

Then the lady, whose name turns out to be Mary the Mags, goes and sits down and asks for a beer. There is a big shout of glee, since the guys have been thinking it is time someone brings the Rox down a notch or two. And she is certainly the first person to do that.

A step too far

They say sharks can smell the blood of a victim from miles away, and I can tell you hawks are much the same. They can spot their prey hundreds of feet below. The smaller bird senses danger but is powerless to escape.

It comes as something of a surprise when I realize the same thing happens with people. Including the Boss. One day, along with the crowds of ordinary people who come to listen, some of the Robed Ones are nosing around. Like sharks smelling blood.

In the beginning they just watch and listen, sizing up their prey. They take notes – and report back to base. Maybe to the army of occupation: more likely just to their own leaders in those early days.

Each time they show up you can feel the tension rising. As though they are trying to trap the Boss into making a mistake or trying to get him to back down; and him not having any of it and going on just the same. Things that seem small and unimportant till you glimpse the hidden meaning. Like a game of chess: move and counter-move.

But the real trouble starts the day the Boss goes mad.

At first nothing special seems to be happening. Some woman is standing at the edge of a cemetery which lies outside the walls of the city; just where the land begins to rise into the hills. Nearby a young man is watching her. Finally she turns and walks away; slowly, as though lost in thought.

As she passes, the man speaks to her.

'Someone special?'

'Yes,' she says. 'But not here. The grave is empty.'

'Empty?'

'The military took him away and we never saw him again. I bought the grave for him, but they never released the body. So I will have it sealed up again. Maybe for me.'

'You loved him?'

'A little. He was special. He wrote things. Dangerous things. A rumour about someone sent by God.'

'That's why I am here,' says the young man. 'He has come: the one who is sent.'

'Where is he?'

'Over there, where the crowds are.'

'You a friend of his?'

'Not yet. I just needed to come here.'

'You are very young. What's your name?'

'John. And you?'

'Liberty.'

The man laughs. 'A good name.'

Together the woman and young John cross the road and join the crowd. The Boss is telling the people how even the poorest of them are loved by God. And the Robed Ones are hanging around on the fringes of the crowd like a bad smell. The sun is hot and a fly is buzzing around.

Suddenly in the distance comes the sound of a bell. Not a clear ringing but a dull, dead clanging. Everyone knows what it means.

Up the road hobbles a bent and ragged creature. Half human, half dead. And the filth: you never saw such filth. In its claws it holds an old piece of rusty iron and is hitting it with a stick. The dull clanging sounds like the passing bell for the dead at a funeral. But no one is dead. Not quite – not yet. Though Jez has a strange look on his face when he hears that sound – as though he is remembering something. Maybe knowing that it tolls for him.

When the crowd realize the leper is coming towards them they back away, leaving the Boss and the boys and Mary the Mags and the young John with open space all around them. And the leper carries on coming.

Under the matted hair, you glimpse a face half missing from the skin being eaten away; and hands twisted into claws like no bird or animal I ever saw.

For a moment I think young John is going to be sick and the Rox says: 'Oh hell.' And Mary the Mags can't help but look away, even though she is a very tough lady.

They all know what leprosy is, but until that moment no one has really understood what it means. Not just the disease destroying the flesh, but the isolation. The crowd backing away in disgust: the bell to warn people not tô come close. A person condemned to a living death by the Robed Ones and their rules that say no one must touch such a person or even go near them.

And for a moment that seems to last for ever everyone stands frozen: not moving. Except the Boss, who has gone mad. He is walking slowly towards the creature holding out his hand and he has a look on his face I never saw before: deep, deep anger. Not at the creature, or the stench that comes from its flesh and its filth, but from the living death imposed upon it.

At first they think Jez is holding out his hand in some sort of prayer or blessing and for a moment no one moves. Then they suddenly realize what is happening. Seeing what the Boss is doing, the creature draws back with a cry of anguish, dropping the stick and the lump of metal in the dust.

The Rox yells a warning, but it is too late. The Boss has reached out and touched the creature; resting his hand gently on its shoulder and quietly drawing the struggling figure towards him. A murmur of horror rises from the crowd and the sharks edge forward to get a clear view of what is going on.

There is a moment of silence and the creature slips to its knees and then speaks in the voice of a human: 'If you wish to, you can make me clean.'

The Boss gives a strange groan and kneels with the creature in the dust. 'I do,' he says, holding the broken figure gently in his arms. 'Be made clean.'

How long they kneel huddled together there in the hot sun and the dust no one can remember. It seems like hours, or it may only be a few moments. It is as though everyone in the crowd is stunned into silence. Finally, Jez gets slowly to his feet, lifting the creature up with him. He pulls back the matted hair which hides the creature's face. And we see that it is a man: whole and unmarked.

A roar of approval goes up from the crowd, but the Rox is yelling at the Boss: 'You're mad, you're mad. Why did you do that? Why did you need to touch him?'

At first I cannot figure out why the Rox is so upset. But then it comes to me: touching the diseased creature, Jez has deliberately made himself unclean under the law of the Robed Ones. As though he, too, has become a leper.

But the Boss seems totally unconcerned. In fact he has that smile on his face that I've seen before; the smile that means something big is going on.

The sharks have also sensed something important is happening because they have quietly pushed through to the front of the crowd and are watching Jez intently. At first they don't get it but then, gradually, they realize what he has done.

Jez has quietly torn up half their rule book. The bit that says only the pure and clean can approach God. The bit that condemns the sinful, whatever that means, to a life of isolation and rejection outside the community.

The Robed Ones turn and walk quickly away and, for a moment, I almost think the Rox is going to follow them. He looks back angrily at the Boss:

'Do you know what you've done? There's going to be big trouble now.'

And for once he is right.

The first casualty

The day begins quietly – apart from an argument the Boss is having with some of the Robed Ones who are unhappy about the way the gang operate.

The Robed Ones are obsessed with rules and regulations. Everything has to be done in a particular way. Maybe it is because they feel insecure. Perhaps it's all pumped up by the fact that the country is run by the occupying forces who are not too sympathetic to local traditions.

Whatever the reason, the Robed Ones believe that people must keep themselves pure at all costs if they want to worship God. Purity is the big thing: so washing, specially before meals, is essential.

This seems strange to me. I eat all sorts of stuff people throw away: so pecking around in the dust must exclude me from whatever it is they are into. No room for sparrows in their heaven. Anyway: these guys live by the book; and they are going to make sure other people do the same.

Except Jez and the gang do not seem to have grasped this.

So here we are on a bright sunny morning with the guys in the black robes banging on about the Boss and the others not washing their hands before they eat and what a big deal this is. They are demanding to know how a man of God can be so ignorant as not to understand that this cleansing is essential.

And the Boss is picking bits of breakfast out of his teeth with a not too clean finger nail and looking bored, like he is thinking of something else. When suddenly, far off in the distance, a bomb goes off.

We all hear the explosion. A dull thud. And then nothing. Moments later I feel the air pressure change for an instant. Then everything is back to normal.

The argument over food continues when, suddenly, there is the sound of a siren and an ambulance roars past followed by two jeeps full of soldiers. They vanish down the road in a cloud of dust.

Of course everybody sets off to see what is happening and, after about a mile, we come on the wreckage of a car near some ruined buildings.

A bomb buried in the road has turned the car inside out. There is charred debris everywhere.

The emergency lights on the ambulance are still flashing, but the occupants of the car were killed instantly in the blast. Sifting through the torn-up steel and charred remains they find TV equipment and realize a group of media people have been the target.

After hanging about for some time, the two jeeps and the ambulance drive off, taking what few bits of identification material they have been able to find. Two soldiers stay to guard the wreckage that still has some dark red paint visible on the blackened bodywork.

While we are standing around, a debate starts about how it is wrong to take out non-combatants. I see the Boss has that look on his face and I know something is going to happen.

He turns to one of the locals and says: 'What was special about these guys?' indicating the burned-out wreck of the Press vehicle.

The local man looks hard at the Boss and says: 'I will tell you a story.

'One day two jeeps show up full of soldiers. Also with them come two big yellow bulldozers that have black writing on them. They come into the village and they start knocking down the houses.

'They smash the place up. They smash up the water supply. They smash up the sewerage system. They tear up the orchards and the olive groves that have been here a thousand years. They destroy the houses where people live all their lives, smashing up all their furniture and their crockery and personal belongings. Many people get out of their houses fast. But some are not so quick. Some people are injured under the walls and the roofs that come down on top of them.

'And the TV cameras are there. But, I ask you, how do the TV people know this village is going to be smashed up and where to take their pictures? How do they know they will not be shot and killed by the army people with the big yellow bulldozers?

'Then we see some kid is lying in the street with blood coming out of his head and his older brother, who is maybe eleven, is trying to pick him up. Finally he manages to carry him towards the road where there might be a car that will take them to a hospital.

'But suddenly an army jeep drives round very fast in a cloud of dust, cutting them off and stopping them getting to the road.

'And the soldiers make the boy stand there in the hot sun with his little brother in his arms. And they are standing there for a long time. But later it turns out that it does not matter, for the little kid is already dead because he has been shot in the back of the head.

'Later, when the TV news is on, it says that the security forces make an incursion into rebel-held areas in the search for suspects. There is a shot of a jeep by the road and the soldiers are having a cigarette and laughing.

'And parked in the sun near one of the bulldozers is a car. And on the side in big white letters it says: TV.'

The Boss is quiet for a few moments.

'Where is this village?' he says to the man.

'You are standing next to it,' he says, looking round at the wasteland by the side of the road. 'The soldiers can do anything because no one knows what they do. The Press people hide the truth. They say their hands are clean, but they are not. There is blood on them. They kill us with their deceit as surely as the men with the guns and the bulldozers. Maybe the journalists who died today were people who spoke the truth; I do not know. But that is why these things happen.'

The Boss looks suddenly at the people who have gathered round while the man has told the story of his village. And the Robed Ones are there too but they are very quiet because they know they are collaborators with the army of occupation and the men with the bulldozers.

'Listen to me,' says Jez with anger in his voice. 'It is not whether you wash your hands or what you eat that defiles you; it is what comes out of your mouth that defiles you and brings death.'

And the people know he is talking about them but also about the Press people who have died and the hundreds of others that work for the big TV networks and newspapers that stop the truth being told and allow the killing and the suffering to happen. Here and in many other places in the world.

'It is the deceit that you speak and the evil in your heart that matters – not the food that you eat,' he says.

And the Robed Ones are furious about this because the Boss is threatening the control system they use to keep people in their place. They know they should be blowing the whistle on the lies that allow the Army and the politicians behind them to get away with murder. But to say anything will mean they are removed from their positions of power.

And the Robed Ones know that the Boss is saying it is not just what comes out of a person's mouth that brings death. It is also what people do not say.

When they stay silent while a village is destroyed and turned into a wasteland and when men with guns make a small boy stand in the hot sun with the body of his dead brother in his arms.

Most deadly weapon

Not many people remember Brother Simon. To someone who has never met him, it may be that his name suggests a guy in a monastery with a very peaceful look on his face and a life dedicated to prayer and contemplation.

However, Simon's only link with the monastic life is the bald patch on the top of his noggin and his resulting nick-name, which is the Monk. And the only contemplation the Monk has done is to quietly think how many of the occupying forces he can get in the sights of his AK47 rifle.

Even now the Monk remains a very excitable character and has real problems with the Boss's rule that people should love their enemies. Nevertheless, he has turned over a new page and has, at least for the time being, relinquished guns and violence towards the occupation forces and the puppet government and the Robed Ones who help to keep the politicians in power.

It is only on this basis that the Boss allows the Monk to join the gang, which is an open gathering of people with no entry qualifications, other than that you do not go around shooting people dead and otherwise harming them.

Not that the Monk ever shoots people for the fun of it. Guys like him would much prefer to have a quiet office job and holidays by the sea. But the way things are, with people being powerless to stop the illegal occupation of their lands and the oppression which drives many of them to an early grave, sometimes the gun seems the only answer.

Someone said it is like a child being strangled by a man. The kid shouts and yells but no one comes to save him. Then the child, who is by now half dead, starts to kick out at the man who is choking him to death in the hope that the man will stop attacking him.

The guy turns and says to people who are passing by: 'See, this is a very violent child who needs a good beating to make him behave.' And the people, who have been watching but doing nothing to save the child, agree that violent children deserve all they get. And they walk away, so they do not see whether the child is left dead or alive.

That is why people like the Monk finally take to the streets with worn-out guns and home-made rocket launchers: because they cannot bear any longer to see their husbands, wives and children strangled to death while the world looks on.

To me it is surprising that the Monk and the other people, who are called the Zealots, are taking to the streets to face the overwhelming power of the Army. But Brother Simon says they have to do something. And in any case it is not the guns the soldiers have that are the problem.

Which may sound a bit strange when people are shooting at you. But Brother Simon has this theory. And when he tells you his theory he is smiling: but it is not a friendly smile. The theory is that every time a gun is fired, a bell rings. Except nobody ever seems to hear the bell ring.

It could be that the guns make so much noise that no one notices the bell; and perhaps that is how it is meant to be. No one is meant to hear the bell in case they start to ask why it is ringing.

And this is the Monk's theory, which is not just about guns, but about all the weapons of mass destruction that we are always hearing about on the TV. He reckons the most deadly weapon of mass destruction ever created has been around for a very long time. The earliest examples of this WMD, he says, were made of brass and very ornate. And every time they were used, a bell rang. Later models were electric and the latest versions are computerized with laser scanners.

When they first hear this the gang are very taken with this theory, which sounds like a riddle, since no one can think of what this weapon of mass destruction can be. Even though the Monk says they have often seen one and that, in fact, there is one right here in the bar where they are drinking at this very moment and there are a load more down the road at the supermarket.

And finally the gang admit that they do not know what sort of a deadly weapon of mass destruction this can be that has killed more men, women and children than any other weapon on the planet. So the Monk tells them the answer: which is a cash register.

This is the most deadly weapon in the world and every time it goes off a bell rings. And the reason it is so deadly, says the Monk, is that every time a gun goes off, some arms manufacturer is making money and some government or other is taking land or some trans-global enterprise is grabbing more resources such as oil or minerals.

And, mostly, that is why wars are fought and people get killed, says the Monk. Because wars are about money and wealth.

And the reason soldiers are given medals and have splendid dress uniforms and military bands play rousing music at parades is because if they didn't, then nobody would be crazy enough to go out and kill other people just to make rich people richer. And often it is the poor who have no jobs who are conned into becoming soldiers.

And the gang are all agreed that such things are very terrible and they are all glad that they do not do such things, and that none of their friends do such evil things either.

But then the Boss says, just hold on a minute. How many of you are tempted by wealth? How many of you are impressed by another person's possessions and judge them by their income? Do you not store up savings and possessions while other people go hungry? Is it not true that you put your trust in money instead of trusting in God – and your lives are ruled by the cash register?

Where your treasure is, there will your heart be also, he tells them. Do you want your heart, your life, to be locked up in a bank vault? How many people have stored up great wealth and thought they would live in luxury for the rest of their days: but then comes a stock market crash, and suddenly they have nothing and there are people jumping to their deaths out of high-rise windows rather than face ruin and disgrace.

This is no way to live, says the Boss. Put your trust in God and share what you have so that everyone can live. And it sounds like he thinks the weapon of mass destruction that the Monk has been speaking of is pretty destructive of ordinary lives.

The Rox, who is very chastened by what the Monk and the Boss have been saying, pledges that he will never go near a cash register again. But the gang say that, on the contrary, he will be going near a cash register very soon if he values his life, on account of how it is his round and many of them cannot remember when he last bought the drinks.

For the rest of the evening the bell on the cash register hardly stops ringing but, under the surface, the gang have heard what the Monk has been saying and they know why he once carried a gun. And, though it is uncomfortable for them, they also hear what the Boss is saying about wealth and possessions.

But, day by day, one person is becoming more and more distanced from the group and from what the Boss is saying. Leaving his half-finished beer on the table, he slips out of the bar and stands outside in the darkness thinking about what he should do. How can he get the Boss to be more reasonable and less extreme? Somehow he needs a jolt to bring him to his senses.

And, very slowly, an idea begins to form in his mind as to how this might happen.

The small freight train

I wish I could tell you it had gone better: with dignity as would befit such an important event. Maybe the most significant thing he ever said. But instead it turns out to be complete chaos – at least at the start.

Often the Boss goes out early in the mornings when it is hardly light. Later, they find him lost in his thoughts, praying. And so it is that, one day, the gang get it into their heads that they want the Boss to teach them how to pray. Not in the old way like the Robed Ones do, but in the way the Boss prays; for they know he has something special going with God and they want to be part of it.

But the Boss seems to think there is no special way to pray and that you just make some space and talk to God and somehow God does the rest. But the gang do not wish to leave it at that and so a lively debate is going on as they are walking down the street in some town or other which I cannot, to be truthful, remember.

Suddenly, running flat-out towards them is a small child with her arms out-stretched and a big beaming smile on her face that seems to light up the street. 'Hey,' says the Rox as the little girl comes steaming along towards the Boss like a small freight train, 'You have a young admirer here.'

And the Boss squats down and holds out his arms towards her in greeting with a big silly grin on his face. But as the small child reaches the Boss she does a neat little swerve and carries on running past him and into the arms of a guy who is walking along some way back.

'Abba, Abba,' she yells as though she has not seen this guy who is her daddy for many years; although it turns out they have only been parted since breakfast time. But for a small child, and many grown ups, that can feel like many years if you love someone a lot.

Meanwhile things are not going so good for the Boss. As the small child hurtles past him she brushes his arm and, because he is squatting down, he loses his balance and goes, wallop, on his backside in the dust. The gang and various onlookers think this is a very funny thing to happen to a guy who is expecting a big hug from a bright young lady. And someone comments that this is often happening to guys who mistake the intentions of ladies and end up on their backsides looking stupid.

But as the Boss scrambles to his feet and bats the dust off his pants, he looks up and sees the other guy hugging the little girl who is still yelling 'Abba, Abba, Daddy, Daddy,' in a very endearing way. And the guy is looking so happy you'd think his heart was going to burst with joy.

Then the Boss gathers the gang round him. 'You want to know how to pray?' he says. 'OK, I will tell you. When you pray you say: Abba.'

There is a somewhat embarrassed silence after this, as the gang expect him to go on and tell them the rest of the prayer. But that is it. Just one word.

And even then they are not happy with the word – or at least young John is not. He thinks the Boss has got a bit confused. The word 'Abba' is a small child sort of word meaning 'Daddy'. So he suggests that the Boss should use the dignified religious word 'Abinu' meaning 'My honoured father' which has been the custom for many centuries.

But the Boss says, no, he has not made a mistake, and the 'Abba' word which the small freight train has been calling out to her dad is exactly the right way to talk to God. And young John is totally amazed at this and is about to argue further when the Rox suddenly chimes in and says he isn't going to say this 'Abba' thing anyway, on account of he is not a child – which makes several of the gang smile since in many ways he is just like a child; except maybe not so bright.

By this time the guy and his daughter have come up and the father is apologizing to Jez for his small child having dumped him on his backside in the dust in front of everyone. But the Boss seems to think it is really funny and how he must remember not to jump to conclusions next time. But, hey, he says, while you are here can I borrow your little girl for a moment?

And he puts his hand on the girl's shoulder and turns to the Rox and says: 'See this young lady? Unless you become like a little child you are never going to enter the Kingdom of Heaven.' By which, they figure out later, he means something like having the trust and honesty of a child and not pretending you are something big, like the Rox is occasionally prone to do.

Meanwhile, young John, who usually seems to know just what the Boss is thinking, is still not comfortable with this new word. And the others are pretty unhappy that they have been told a prayer that is only one word long, while most normal prayers the Robed Ones say go on for so long you can fall asleep part way through and wake up later and they still have not finished.

So the next day they go back and ask for more words.

But the Boss is not feeling very co-operative, for he asks them whether they have prayed the 'Abba' word yet. And young John has to admit he cannot get his head round the idea that you can talk to the maker of heaven and earth in such a familiar way. So the Boss asks whether John knows how much God loves people, and whether or not it might be like the guy in the street loves the small freight train.

And they all gradually get to thinking that the childish 'Abba' word may not be so stupid after all; although they are still amazed that the whole of this thing with God can be summed up in a word that a kid of three knows how to say. But the Mags is grumbling that it ought to be 'Ammu' and not 'Abba' and everybody is then wanting to know what the hell 'Ammu' means. And it turns out it means 'Mummy' and the Mags wants to know why it is always all about men.

At this point the Boss suddenly decides that maybe there are more words in the prayer after all, and they should say: 'Abba. Your name be hallowed. Your kingdom come.'

And the guys – and even the Mags – think this is OK because they know they should always respect and reverence the presence and the nature of God and do what he wants, which is about love and justice: which is all they have so far managed to figure out about this Kingdom.

And young John has an odd look on his face like he is thinking deep things and he suddenly says: 'Hallowed be your name. Hallowed be your neighbour. Love God: love your neighbour.'

And the Boss laughs as though he thinks that is not far off the mark after all. But the rest of the gang do not know what young John is on about and get a bit cross and start saying to the Boss that, OK, they now have a prayer with eight words in it, but that is still a somewhat short prayer and maybe there should be some more.

But the Boss thinks that if they can pray those eight words, and mean what they say, they will be doing pretty well. And maybe it will take them some time to work through what those eight words mean. What he doesn't say is that eight words is about all some of them can remember anyway.

But he knows they are never going to shut up about this matter and says that perhaps he will have a think and maybe come up with some more words; but only if they can remember, off by heart, the eight he has already told them.

And then they start arguing among themselves about just what the eight words were; and the Boss goes and sits in a chair in the sun. He leans back and closes his eyes and smiles. And pretty soon he is asleep.

Unexpected rescue

One hot day the Boss and the others are relaxing under the awning of a roadside café, having a few beers and thinking about what they might do next, when a shadow suddenly falls across the proceedings. A shark is nosing around. At once the general chat stops and there is an uneasy silence.

I am up in the shade where the awning meets the roof when I hear the voices suddenly go quiet, and I take a look to see what is happening. Sure enough there is one of the Robed Ones, looking like an old crow with his beard and screwed-up face, which has so many wrinkles you can hardly see where his eyes are.

The guys get a bit agitated when the old one shows up, since they remember how much trouble these characters in their black robes cause the Boss.

Anyway, the shark glides quietly up till he is near the table where the Boss is sitting with a half-empty glass resting on a copy of the day's paper. And it is clear he has come for a purpose.

'Can I ask you a question?' he says.

'Sure,' says Jez, who is not looking at all worried.

The old man says: 'Which is the greatest commandment of God?'

There is a moment's silence as each person tries to figure out what the game is. The Robed Ones always try to set a trap – usually with a question. The trick is to work out where the trap is.

But Jez doesn't seem to be interested in playing games. Instead he sits forward in his chair and looks right into the eyes of the Robed One; and when he starts to speak his voice has that edge that makes you think this is the most important question that has ever been asked. And maybe it is.

The Boss says: 'The first commandment is this. "You shall love the Lord your God with all your heart and with all your soul and with all your mind, and with all your strength."'

And then he goes on: 'And the second commandment is: "You shall love your neighbour as you love yourself." There are no other commandments greater than these.'

The old man looks at the Boss and, for a moment, you think these guys are on the same waveband. But then he asks another question: is this the trap being set?

'Who is my neighbour?' he says. And he looks round at the guys and at the Mags and the other women as if to say: 'Are these people my neighbour?'

Jez picks up his glass and takes a slow pull at the beer. Then he takes the newspaper from the table and starts to read aloud from an article: 'A man was travelling out of the city on the desert road yesterday when his car came under attack from rebels.'

He glances up at Andy as though a thought has just occurred to him: 'Here, you tell him the story,' he says, and passes the newspaper across.

Andy takes the paper and studies the article. After a few moments he bursts out laughing. Finally he puts the paper down and looks across at Jez with a grin on his face.

'OK, now tell the rest of us the story,' says the Boss patiently.

'Well,' says Andy, looking round the assembled group to make sure he has their attention. 'The guy in the car is none other than one of our friends, the Robed Ones. Suddenly, what should happen next but one of those bad rebel people jumps up out of the ditch at the side of the road and takes a pop at him with a rocket launcher. Wham!

'The rocket hits the car but it fails to explode. Instead it smashes into the front suspension.

'The Robed One loses control and the car plunges off the road, demolishes a fence and ends up in a field. There is a bloody big bang and the car turns over on its side, depositing him in the dust with a broken arm and many other injuries.'

'Pity it wasn't a broken neck,' says a voice from the back.

'So what happens next?' says Andy sternly to reassert his authority. 'Another car comes down the road driven by another of our robed friends. But when he sees the smashed-up car in the field, he takes fright and leaves in a cloud of dust, never to be seen again.

'Time passes and the sun is getting hotter and the guy in the smashed-up car is no doubt feeling very unhappy by now. But then comes another car – this time driven by one of our military friends. He, too, sees the wreck and just for a moment it seems he might stop and help. But, no. He also has a pressing engagement somewhere – anywhere but here where there might be rebels with rocket launchers. And he also disappears.

'By now the injured guy is all but dead, when suddenly a third car heaves into view. It's a battered old Toyota being driven by a woman with a lot of schlap on her face and not many clothes on the rest of her. And guess what she does for a living.'

Andy holds up the paper to reveal a picture of a young woman. There are shouts of approval from the men and someone yells: 'A hooker! She'll sort him out!'

'You're damn right there,' says Andy. 'The car stops. The young woman looks across at the wreck and the Robed One lying bleeding in the dust. Then she takes off her shades, lights a cigarette and sits as if trying to make up her mind about something. She looks at a sign at the roadside and then across to the injured man again.

'Finally she gets out of the rusty old Toyota, chucks her fag away and takes off her high-heels.

'Then she walks slowly across the field towards the wrecked car. At first the Robed One seems horrified that she is a prostitute and that she is going to touch him. But then he realizes she's his best chance of staying alive and decides to button his lip.

'Anyway, what does the young woman do but grab the collar of his black robe, drag him back to the road and heave him across the back seat of the car. Then she goes to find her heels. Going back to the car she glances at the little sign at the side of the road.

'The sign says: "Danger: Landmines."

'She lights another cigarette, then she takes her sunglasses out of her white shoulder bag and puts them on. And then she drives off to get the injured guy fixed.'

There is silence round the table.

'So who was neighbour to the guy in the car?' says Jez to the old man in the robes.

'Young man,' says the Robed One, 'you have great wisdom. You are right: nothing matters more than to love God with all our heart and with all our understanding and with all our strength; and to love our neighbour as ourselves.'

The Boss smiles. He reaches out and gives the old man's hand a gentle squeeze. 'My friend,' he says, 'you are not far from the Kingdom.'

Opposing forces

It is a strange start to the day as a scream shatters the silence of the dawn. It wakes me instantly. For a few seconds there is quiet; then a sudden uproar from inside the house as Jez and the others rush noisily upstairs to the room where the Mags is sleeping.

Crashing through the door, they find her pressed with her back against the wall. She is staring in terror at the floor on the opposite side of the bedroom. The gang look around the room, but no one is there. Just a spider.

Young John, who is nearest, scoops up the intruder and walks swiftly out of the room with cupped hands. Andy makes the mistake of laughing and passing a thoughtless comment about women but he is silenced by a slap across the face. The Mags is recovering rapidly.

Breakfast is eaten in an uncomfortable silence. Then, once more, they are on the road.

From high above I can see the people moving purposefully towards the gang like a procession of ants. At first small groups but, as the morning goes on, these become crowds of hundreds – maybe thousands. And all of them are trying to get to Jez, and all want one thing. Healing.

What happens with this healing thing, no one knows. They come from the towns and the villages; the houses, the hovels and the desert caves. They say they are cursed. Cursed with many things: possession; demons; spirits; blindness; paralysis. Despair.

The Rox calls it the Darkness. 'Why is this happening?' he asks young John. 'Why should ordinary, normal people believe they are possessed; and certainly behave as though they are? What's happening to them?'

Young John's theory is that the people have their heads in the jaws of an enormous vice: caught between the army of occupation and the puppet government of the Robed Ones; taxed so savagely that they lose houses, fields and possessions until they are destitute. Trapped between hopeless rebellion and total despair, many of them seem to go insane.

Children suddenly go blind or become paralysed as mental and emotional circuits trip out. Kids who have seen school-friends shot in the street by army snipers, or who have seen their homes demolished and their parents humiliated, lapse into a silent hysteria. Bed-wetting. Epilepsy. Withdrawal into an inner world. Self-harm. Slashed wrists. Suicide. A tide of despair gradually swallowing up the hope of the people, says John.

The Boss is strangely silent as he listens to what John is saying. It is as though he is carrying a great weight. Or maybe waiting for the coming tide of suffering to reach him.

People carried on stretchers; people bent and lame; people who have gone blind for no apparent reason. He speaks gently and urgently, though his words seem lost in the growing clamour of the crowd.

Another damaged person approaches, shouting wildly: 'I know you. I know you. What have you to do with us? Get away from us. Go away. I know who you are: you are the Holy One of God. You are the Son of the Most High.'

But the man's eyes are somewhere else and the Boss can see that the words are also coming from somewhere else; as though a great struggle is going on inside him. Suddenly the man collapses.

His friends and the Boss kneel beside him in the dust until, at last, he appears to recover. 'Now go back to your village,' says Jez. 'Show them that you are well.'

Still they come – in their hundreds: wave after wave of bewildered suffering humanity, flooding round the Boss in the hot mid-day sun. And he touches them and speaks to them; and something seems to happen and they are changed.

People watching are amazed at what is happening, until one of them, a woman standing next to young John, says: 'He speaks with authority.'

It is as though the Boss hears what the woman has said, for he looks across the crowd at her and for a moment it seems there is silence. Then he turns back to the people and carries on speaking and touching; speaking and touching, until you think he will drop down dead from exhaustion.

But young John has heard what the woman says about the Boss. 'What did you mean about authority?' he asks.

She smiles. 'You are his friend. Don't you know?'

John looks embarrassed: 'Tell me,' he says. 'Why does authority matter? He's healing people – that's what matters.'

She smiles again and puts her hand on his arm. 'Healing people? That's only a small part of what's happening. What is damaging these people is an alien and overwhelming power.'

'So?' says John.

'Don't you see? He speaks with an authority that is greater than the Army and the Robed Ones. He has an authority that is above the forces that oppress them. By his actions he's telling them that. He's saying that the love of God is greater and more powerful than all the tanks and bulldozers. He's giving them hope. That hope is what is making those people whole again.

'Each person who is healed is a sign that something greater is here. This man is fighting a war: a war of non-violence. A war that tells us to love our enemy; but not to be crushed by what that enemy does to us.'

'But why does he send the people home afterwards? Why doesn't he tell them to follow us and help us fight this war?' says John in exasperation.

The woman smiles again: 'A bit slow, aren't you! Subversion. Ripples on a pond. He sends them back to their homes and families so other people can see what has happened. So that maybe they will glimpse that there is a greater authority and power than the oppressor. And the word will spread and the spirit of the people will not be broken. And the darkness your friend talks about will leave us.

'Anyway – he sends them away because he does not want to control them. He wants them to be free. Isn't that what God's love means? Freedom for the oppressed?'

By now the crowd has thinned and the gang are moving on to try to find shelter for the night. There's a chill in the air. It's been a long day.

'Who are you, anyway?' says John, suddenly aware that they will probably never meet again.

'Sophie.'

'Sophie? That's a good name for you,' says John, laughing. 'Like Sophia: wisdom.'

The woman smiles.

Meanwhile there is a discussion going on about the wild man who shouted abuse at the Boss – yelling for him to go away.

'Maybe something in the man recognized who Jez is and found it a threat,' says Sophie. 'A bit like when you can sense something you are really scared of. I know someone who has a thing about spiders.'

The Mags and young John glance at each other. 'Who is this?' says the Mags quietly.

'Don't know,' says John, 'but I hope she sticks around.'

'Me too,' says the Mags.

The man who grew carrier bags

Of all the meals they have had, few can compare with the upside down dinner. Permanently hungry, the gang are mesmerized by the size of the huge round cooking pan which it takes two men to carry to the table. And they are even more enthralled when the pan is deftly turned upside down and the contents of chicken, rice, nuts and spices emerge as a steaming mountain of delicious food: magically still in the round shape of the pan.

For the next hour thirty people sit and eat and drink till no one can manage another grain of rice or piece of chicken. Yussuf's young wife is toasted as the most wonderful cook they have ever known. As the meal comes to an end, dark-eyed children suddenly appear and stare shyly at the visitors who have come to their village.

'How many children have you, Yuss?' asks the Boss.

Yuss smiles with contentment. 'Children?' he says. 'I have many, many children. Maybe seventy or eighty children.'

There is an embarrassed silence as the gang realize there has been a slight misunderstanding.

'No,' says young John helpfully. 'How many children do you have?'

Yuss continues to smile broadly, enjoying the situation. 'Yes, maybe seventy or eighty. Three boys and two girls – and then the others. Many others.'

'Others?' says the Boss warily. 'What others are there, Yuss?'

'Come outside and I will show you,' says Yuss, and he leads the gang out of the back of the house to a large field on the rocky hillside.

'My other children,' he says proudly pointing to a grove of olive trees. 'Some are grown-up children. Some were my father's children.

Some, my grandfather's children. Some are hundreds of years old, but they are my children – they are my family. And one day they will be my children's children, and my grandchildren's children.'

There is a murmur of gentle laughter at the joke which was not a joke because it is, in a way, true; and they all go back into the large single room of the house for another drink and a cigarette.

The memory of that happy evening stays with the gang for many months after that as they travel on; especially when times get tough and there is not so much in the way of food. And the smell of Mrs Yussuf's cooking is a distant but wonderful memory.

So it comes as no surprise that the gang are immensely cheered by the news that now, almost a year later, we are passing that way again and word is being sent on ahead to Mr Yuss that another upside down chicken and rice special would not by any means be an unwelcome thing.

And so, after a long trek in the dust and the sun, the gang are now on the outskirts of the village of Mr Yuss and his wonderful wife; and the boys comment on how they can almost smell the grub cooking and how Mr Yuss is certainly the luckiest person on this earth.

But as they enter the village there is some slight confusion as to where the house of Mr Yuss is located. The street which the Boss feels sure is the right address somehow looks different from a year ago. Not least because there has been some major demolition work going on. Finally they locate the place where the house is. Only to find a huge pile of rubble and dust.

In the distance they can see an old man stooping over some twigs that are stuck in the ground. On the twigs, flapping in the wind, are bits of coloured plastic carrier bags. The man turns slowly, as if in a dream. He sees the Boss and the gang, but he does nothing. He just stands there in the dust among the wildly flapping plastic carrier bags he has been planting in rows as though they are a grove of olive trees.

And the Boss goes and takes Mr Yuss by the hand and leads him gently away from the flapping bags and holds him in his arms. And then a woman appears from one of the nearby houses and we see it is none other than Mrs Yuss; but she does not look so good these days and she will not be doing any cooking, because her home and her cooker and the big pan she cooks the upside down chicken and rice in, is all smashed flat by the bulldozers that come in the night with their headlights on.

The people are given five minutes to get out of the house. But in the dark they cannot find the two little girls who are scared to leave the safety of the house because of the men with the guns and the deafening roar of the bulldozers. And so they are crushed beneath the rubble and it is three days before their bodies are found and brought out.

The Boss is very quiet and then says: 'Three days?'

And Mrs Yuss says: Yes, it is three days because there is a curfew for that three days and anyone who goes into the street or tries to dig in the rubble during that time will be shot by the occupation forces who are controlling the area. And when the three days are past, the little girls are dead.

Meanwhile the bulldozers rip up all the trees in the olive grove at the back of the house where Mr Yuss and his wife live until the area is a wasteland like the desert. And the gang remember that these also are the children of Mr Yuss.

For a moment I think the Boss is going to explode, he is so angry. And it is as though if he meets one of the armour-plated bulldozers right now he will destroy it just with the fury that is raging within him. But instead the Boss asks everyone to sit down and to listen really good.

And he still has his arm round the old man who last year was Mr Yuss. Then he starts to speak and his voice is so hard you think you are being hit with a hammer:

'Blessed are you that weep now,' he says to Mr Yuss. 'For you shall laugh.

'Blessed are you that go hungry now, for you shall be filled.'

He is silent for a moment. Then he lifts his eyes as if to include the gang and the neighbours of Mr Yuss who have now gathered round: 'Blessed are you who are oppressed and impoverished now, for yours is the Kingdom of God.'

And all the time his voice is getting louder and stronger.

Now he is looking straight at the gang and he says: 'Blessed are you when men hate you and exclude you and revile you on account of the Son of Man – for so their fathers did just that to the prophets.'

At first the gang do not understand what all this is about, but pretty soon they realize he is warning about what is to come for them, like it has come for Mr Yuss. And he is giving them the strength maybe to face up to what is going to happen.

But the Boss is still speaking – and this time he is looking out beyond the gang and Mr Yuss and Mrs Yuss and their neighbours who have also had their houses bulldozed into rubble. He is looking into the far distance as if he is talking to the Robed Ones and to the soldiers and to the powerful people who give orders to the Army.

And half sad and half angry he says: 'But you who are rich and powerful: you have had all you are getting. You that are full now will go hungry. You who laugh now; you will weep.'

And it sounds less like a curse than like a terrible statement of fact.

And some of the gang are all for making contact with the resistance fighters and mounting a counter-attack on the occupying forces to make up for the terrible things that have happened to Mr Yuss and his children and to his neighbours.

But the Boss is not for doing this in any way and, instead, he is talking quietly to his friend Mr Yuss.

And he says to Mr Yuss very gently that it is time now to stop planting carrier bags for, even with the wonderful cooking of Mrs Yuss, they will not taste so good.

Then, for the first time in almost a year, Mr Yuss smiles a little and the wild look in his eyes seems for a moment to be not so wild. And it seems like there may, after all, be more children where the olive grove used to be. And one day there may even be laughter.

Because Mr Yuss remembers somewhere somebody saying to him: 'Yours is the Kingdom of God.'

And, while he has no idea what this Kingdom can be, he somehow thinks that maybe there will be pans of chicken and rice so big that it takes two people to carry them and which even thirty hungry visitors cannot eat at one sitting.

So, even though his heart is broken for the children who have died, he will go and start pulling up all the plastic carrier bag bushes out of which not even the very wonderful Mrs Yuss can make a good meal.

And perhaps one day he will plant more olive trees as a sign to the men who drive the bulldozers that there is life in this place.

The onion carrier

There is no doubt that Andreas the gardener grows the best onions in the world. At least, that is what people hereabouts will tell you. But in his heart the old man knows this is not true and it is his pride that keeps him from admitting his secret.

For many years his onions were the most wonderful anyone had ever tasted but, ever since the pains in his back started and the joints in his hands got swollen and stiff, he has not been able to work in his market garden. Which is strange, since many people say that his onions are better now than they have ever been.

What they do not know is that, since his back gets so bad that he walks doubled over, it is his wife Maria who does the gardening. But he is too proud to tell people what has happened. And she loves him too much to give away his secret. In any case, she says, it is Andreas who shows her how to grow the onions in the first place; so it is as though he is still growing them.

And Andreas and his wife Maria have a good system going for them. Each summer they harvest the onions and take them to the market. And this year is no different.

One fine morning they fill a large sack with onions and tie it with string. Then Maria lifts the heavy sack of onions onto the handle-bars of the ancient black bicycle which is almost as old as Andreas himself. And, carefully, they wheel the old bicycle down to the end of the lane to the place where the bus stops.

When the bus comes, the driver helps them load the heavy sack of onions into the bus which will take Andreas seven miles along the dusty road, through the army checkpoint and across the military highway. Half a mile further on, his nephew will meet him with his rusty red pick-up truck.

Then he and his nephew will drive to the city where Andreas will sell his onions in the market. And after that they will sit and talk and drink glasses of cold beer until it is time to go home.

But today there is a problem. As the bus reaches the military checkpoint, the road is blocked by a large pile of earth and rocks that the soldiers have made with their bulldozer.

Instead of waving the bus through the checkpoint, one of the soldiers jumps on board and tells the passengers they must all get out and walk. No traffic is being allowed to cross the military highway. As they get off the bus into the hot sun, the driver is ordered to turn round and go back the way he came.

The passengers, who happen to include the Boss and several of the gang, are herded like cattle into a concrete enclosure where they have to wait to get their identity cards checked. But Andreas is left standing in the road with his onions.

For a few moments nothing happens. Then there is a shout from the military checkpoint: 'Hey. Old man. Move your sack. You are blocking the road.'

Andreas tries to move the sack of onions but it is too heavy.

'Now,' shouts a menacing voice from the checkpoint. 'Move it now.'

Andreas shrugs and shakes his head.

Suddenly a shot rings out and the old man falls down on top of the sack.

A young soldier walks slowly towards him. 'Next time I will not fire over your head. Now, get up.'

The old man slowly gets to his feet, frightened but unhurt.

'What is in the sack?'

'Onions.'

'Onions? Are you sure it is not weapons?'

'It is onions. This is my country. We have lived here for thousands of years. Am I not allowed to carry onions?'

73

The soldier ignores the question: 'Why did you not move it when I ordered you?'

'It is too heavy.'

The young soldier laughs. 'Well, old man. We will help you. We will make your sack less heavy.'

He turns and whistles to the other soldiers who are standing smoking under the awning of the checkpoint: 'Hey. Over here. Free onions.'

Saying this, he unties the sack. Onions spill into the road.

From the concrete holding pen the Boss and the other passengers from the bus watch as the soldier ties up the sack again, while the others pick up the stolen onions and carry them back to the checkpoint.

'OK,' says the soldier. 'Now I will help you again. And I will make you a promise. I will put the sack of onions on your back and you will carry them. And I promise that, if you stop, I will shoot you.'

'Where am I to walk?' says the old man.

'On your journey. Along this road. Across the military highway. I do not care where you are going with your onions. Just go. Now.'

Andreas staggers under the sudden weight as the soldier picks up the heavy sack and dumps it across his shoulders. Then the old man sets off slowly along the road, bowed down under the weight of the onions, and because his back is bad.

'Remember my promise,' shouts the young soldier laughing again. 'Do not stop.'

It is almost an hour before the Boss and the others are allowed through the checkpoint. As they come out of the interrogation area there is no sign of the old man.

'Wait for me,' he says to the gang, and sets off down the road at a run.

When he finally reaches the wide military highway the old man is standing alone at the roadside. He turns as he hears the Boss approach.

'Can you help me?' he says. 'I cannot get across the road. The traffic comes too fast. The people do not slow down. They laugh and shout as though they want to scare me. Or maybe kill me.'

The Boss takes the sack and heaves it onto his shoulder. Then, holding the old man's arm, they cross the road that is reserved for the army of occupation and their important friends. And even then the cars and trucks that come by do not slow down and many drivers shout and sound their horns.

As they walk the Boss is thinking how other people, young and old, are being made to walk with all their luggage and goods through the bushes and rocks, round the roadblock and then maybe half a mile to the military highway. And then cross the busy road with traffic that does not slow down; and how bad that will be in the rain and in the cold and dark of winter.

'Are you OK?' asks the old man, aware that the Boss has not spoken for some time.

'I am OK. I am thinking how heavy onions are.'

'Maybe it is a good job the soldiers stole some.'

'They are not that heavy.'

'You are young.'

'I am not that young,' says the Boss.

'It is not far now. I can see my nephew's truck down the road.'

Suddenly a young man is running towards them. The sack of onions is thrown gratefully into the back of the pick-up and the three stand sharing a bottle of water in the hot sun.

The Boss is smiling to himself.

'What is funny?' asks the old man.

'Something I said to some friends the other day,' replies the Boss. 'About the task I give them being easy and my burden on them, light. And I am thinking it is lighter than onions. And then I said to them: "Come to me all you who are heavy laden and I will refresh you." But it is you who have refreshed me with this water; and with your company.'

'Maybe you make their burden seem light because you bring them joy,' says the old man. 'Or maybe it is hope you bring, for the people are all bowed down like me. We cannot stand up straight under the burden that is placed on us.'

They finish the water and the Boss says he needs to go find his friends who were on the bus with him.

The old man's nephew helps Andreas into the truck and then turns to the Boss: 'If ever I can be of service to you, let me know,' he says, shaking his hand.

As they drive away, the young man glances across at Andreas. 'You OK?'

'Half my onions are stolen, but I am OK,' says the old man. 'And the pain in my back does not seem so bad.'

The child that died

It has to be said that life is good for some people, even under the Occupation. And for Mr Jenkins-Russell life is extremely good. But Mr Jenkins-Russell had better enjoy the good life while he can, for things are about to fall apart in a big way.

For now, however, all is peace and tranquillity as Mr Jenkins-Russell sits at his polished oak dining table reading the morning paper and sharing an occasional agreeable observation on life with the very agreeable Mrs Jenkins-Russell, who is sitting opposite him. There is no doubting that, since they were married fifteen years ago, fortune has smiled on both of them.

Few of the Robed Ones have made a more effortless progress up the hierarchy than Mr Jenkins-Russell. And few, it has to be said, enjoy more the many benefits that high office brings. Mr Jenkins-Russell not only takes great pleasure in the fine robes he is entitled to wear and the handsome house in which he is entitled to live; but, most of all, he takes pleasure in impartially dispensing the religious law – which is binding on all.

And if that law sometimes seems harsh, this is not a matter that deeply concerns our venerable friend. Until today.

As he takes another bite of toast and marmalade, Mr Jenkins-Russell becomes aware that his daughter, Rebecca Jane, has still not appeared for breakfast. With a slight sigh of disapproval he comments to his wife that at this rate their much loved twelve-year-old will be late for school.

As Mrs Jenkins-Russell goes to investigate the delay, her husband reflects with pleasure on their daughter who is in all respects a perfect child. All respects but one, that is.

That one imperfection is, of course, that she is a girl. All men hope for a son and heir and Mr Jenkins-Russell is no exception. For many years now they have hoped for other children but none has appeared, and now it seems that time has run its course. Even so, few children are loved with more devotion than Rebecca Jane who is, most certainly, her daddy's little girl.

But Mr Jenkins-Russell's quiet reverie is suddenly shattered by a terrible scream from the floor above. A bedroom door bangs as it is thrown open. Mr Jenkins-Russell leaps up from his chair and dashes into the hall, in time to see his wife stumbling down the stairs.

Wild-eyed, she can hardly speak the terrible words: 'She's dead.'

Although medical services are hard to come by in these troubled times, in less than fifteen minutes a doctor is at the Jenkins-Russell residence. For a long time he stoops over the still figure of the little girl. Finally, he turns to the distraught parents. She is not dead but she is dying. She has perhaps an hour. There is no hope: nothing can be done.

Meanwhile, down on the lakeside, the Boss is having his own problems. The crowds are so large that he cannot make himself heard as he stands among them. Finally, he gets into a boat with two of the gang and rows out onto the lake to speak to them.

Suddenly there is a commotion. A man is fighting his way through the crowd as if his life depends on it. Reaching the water's edge he stands shrieking at the Boss – though what he is saying, no one can tell.

Carefully Andy and the Rox row the boat back to the beach and the Boss steps ashore where Mr Jenkins-Russell is shouting and raving as though he has gone out of his head. Suddenly the effort seems too much for him and he crumples to his knees in the dust in despair.

It takes young John and the Mags a couple of minutes to haul the plump Mr Jenkins-Russell to his feet and for him to tell the Boss how his daughter is dying and that he must come right now and try to save her.

The Boss has a thoughtful look on his face when he hears this; maybe because the Robed Ones are spending a lot of time these days trying to get him arrested. And now here is one of them begging him for help.

But the Boss, who is a most forgiving and amiable guy, agrees to go to the house to see what can be done. And to this end they start pushing and shoving their way back through the crowd.

It is at this moment, however, that something very strange happens. Instead of following Mr Jenkins-Russell, who is ploughing ahead through the crowds, the Boss stops and turns round.

'Who touched me?' he says, looking at the faces in the crowd. 'Somebody touched me. Who was it?'

Young John, who is right beside him, says: 'Hey Boss, what is this "touched me" thing? Dozens of people are touching you in this crush. And what does it matter anyhow? We have to go see this child who is on the point of death; so let us get moving.'

By now Mr Jenkins-Russell is shouting like his lungs will burst that there is no time to waste and how his baby is dying. But the Boss, for some crazy reason, will not budge.

Then a woman pushes through the crowd and says to the Boss: 'I touched you. For twelve years, ever since I grew up, I have a terrible leaking of blood that means I cannot work and I cannot have children. No man will marry me because the religious law says I am unclean. All my life I am disgraced. My family are ashamed of me. I have spent all my money on doctors, but it is no good. Now I am penniless and I want to die.

'Then I hear of you and I think, "If I just touch his sleeve as he goes by, maybe I will be made well and freed from this living death." So I touched you.'

At this the Boss looks at her very kindly as though he, too, is almost in tears and he holds her in his arms for a long time like a mother comforts a child. Then, speaking loud so the whole crowd will hear, he says: 'My daughter, your faith has made you well. Go in peace: you are freed from this disease.' And maybe he is thinking she is also freed from this religious baloney that is laid on people by the Robed Ones.

While all this is going on, Mr Jenkins-Russell is screaming for the Boss to stop wasting time and saying that he can come back another time and talk to this woman. And what do women matter anyway? And the gang, who are greatly embarrassed by this needless delay, are in agreement with that, and are tugging at the Boss to get moving.

Then, suddenly, a mobile phone goes off.

Mr Jenkins-Russell snaps open the phone and puts the mobile to his ear. It is a short message. The next moment he hurls the phone to the ground and with a terrible howl like a dog that is dying he launches himself at the Boss as if he is going to strangle him.

'Dead,' he is howling. 'My baby is dead.'

But now the Boss is grabbing him by the front of his robes and giving him a big shaking and when he finally stops yelling he tells him: where is your faith? Do not be afraid. And together they carry on walking to the house of Mr Jenkins-Russell, followed by the gang who are very unhappy at the way the Boss has mis-handled this situation, since they are now hearing from other people that the little girl really is dead.

And when they get to the big house where the Jenkins-Russells live, there is even more trouble. Mrs Jenkins-Russell and many of her family and friends who have shown up are all crying and yelling because the child has died; and at first they will not let the Boss go in. They want to know what took him so long. And anyway they don't want him near them because he has been touching this woman with the leakage of blood and so he also is unclean as far as the religious law of the Jenkins-Russells is concerned. And the law is the law.

But the Boss says the child is not dead but is only asleep. At this the family go crazy with anger and say they will kill him, but the Boss shoves his way through and goes up the stairs with young John and Mr Jenkins-Russell. As he goes he tells the mourners to stop yelling and spitting at him and to put the damn kettle on.

For a few minutes nothing happens. Then there is a great shout from inside the house and suddenly the Boss is walking down the stairs with a very nice-looking little girl who cannot figure out what all the din is about. But Mr Jenkins-Russell is not there, on account of he is flat on his back on the bedroom floor, spark out in a faint because the daughter who was dead is alive.

And maybe when he wakes up he will think about another daughter who was dead and is alive. And he may even think how strange it is that she was dead for twelve years under his harsh religious law, while his own beloved child lived a life of privilege and luxury for that same twelve years in the same town on the lakeside. And that many times they must have passed in the street. One dead and one alive.

And later we hear that Mr and Mrs Jenkins-Russell are not so fussy these days about living in a posh house, and Mr Jenkins-Russell has even started asking awkward questions about the religious laws. And it is felt by those who know such things that he may not be moving any further up the hierarchy after all.

The income tax ambush

One day I will be famous. For, after years of keen observation, I have invented a new law. It may be most people have not yet heard of Sparrow's Law, which is a pity since it applies to them. Sparrow's Law states that the stupidity of a bird is directly proportional to the richness of its plumage. Put simply: fine feathers mean brainless birds.

Think about it: parrots are a great example. Lots of colour but nothing going on upstairs. Of course they can learn to talk – copying what their owners say. But if they had half a brain cell they'd be working out how to get out of the cage rather than performing tricks for a handful of muesli every day. No flying around in the sunshine; no sex; no freedom. Who's a pretty boy? Who's a blockhead, more like.

Peacocks are even worse. Flouncing around looking grand: but have you ever heard one sing? One took a stroll through the village the other day and ended up sitting on some guy's chimney. It thought it was really clever until the man realizes his house is filling up with smoke: so he gets his twelve-bore and goes out into the garden and shoots it. Blam! One shot. And the peacock comes down off that roof like a sack of potatoes. Not so proud and swishy now, Mr Peacock. And the guy picks him up by his fine feathery tail and chucks him in the wheelie bin. And the wheelie bin is empty so the peacock hits the bottom of the big green bin with a loud thud.

Some of you may disagree, but there is an uncanny correlation between the finery people wear and their brain activity. Take, as an example, the memorable incident of the Income Tax Ambush.

Once more the Robed Ones were out to get the Boss and had set up what was for him a no-win situation. Half-way through a conversation with a crowd of people, four of the Robed Ones suddenly show up in their expensive gear. The crowd parts to let them through and they confront the Boss.

One of them, who is obviously the leader and who has even more gold trimmings on his robes than the others, comes up to the Boss and says: 'Teacher, we know you are a man of God and know many things. Tell us this: is it right to pay taxes to the army of occupation or not?'

This is a very tricky question and there is a murmuring in the crowd as people consider the trap that has been laid for the Boss. For if he says it is not right to pay taxes to the oppressors of the people, the Robed Ones are going to go and report him to the military. And if he says, 'Yes, it is right to pay taxes to the occupying forces,' then it will be seen as a betrayal of the people.

But from where I am sitting I can see the Boss has already clocked this and he has that slightly thoughtful look on his face. The one that means trouble. Then, suddenly, he grins.

'Show me a coin,' he tells the one in the fancy robes.

Now the Robed One does not like the sound of this at all. He is very attached to money and handing over even a small coin is not an attractive prospect. But the crowd are now pressing in and there is a lot of excitement around. As if the Boss is going to do some sort of conjuring trick.

So the Robed One pulls out a coin and hands it very slowly to the Boss as though he wishes he had it on a piece of elastic that would somehow pull it back into his pocket at any moment. But the Boss isn't after his money: in fact the Boss is alarmingly uninterested in acquiring money – and that has been a cause of considerable unease among the gang. But that is another story.

Anyway, the Boss takes the coin and looks at it as though he has never seen such a thing before. Then he holds it up for the crowd to see. And all the time the tension is building up and people are wondering how the Boss is going to get out of what has become a very effective ambush.

Then the Boss says to the one in the fancy robes, 'Whose face is it on the coin?'

'It is the face of the Commander in Chief,' says the Robed One.

'Oh, that's OK then,' says the Boss, sounding relieved.

'What do you mean?' says the Robed One suspiciously.

'Well, it's simple,' says the Boss. 'You pay to the Commander in Chief what is due to him. And you pay to God what is due to God.'

The Boss is smiling – and the crowd start laughing. But the Robed One cannot see what is so funny. And he's getting angry because he doesn't know what is going on.

'You're saying it is OK to pay the authorities what is due to them?' he says.

'Absolutely,' says the Boss. 'And to God what is due to God.'

'Is that it?' says the Robed One, mystified.

'That's it,' says the Boss.

By now the crowd are roaring with laughter at the Robed One. But he does not see the funny side of this situation at all.

Then some woman in the crowd finally lets him into the secret.

She shouts out: 'And what is due to God?'

And someone else shouts back: 'Everything. Everything in the earth belongs to the Lord who made the stars in the sky and holds the world in his hands.'

'And what is due to the army of occupation?' shouts the wise woman.

Right on cue comes back the reply: 'What's due to them is a kick up the backside.'

The whole crowd collapse in laughter. People are jumping up and down cheering and the Boss has a big grin on his face and the Robed Ones look as though they are going to commit murder. Which maybe they are.

The Boss says to the man in the fine robes: 'Here is your coin.'

And the Robed Ones glare at the crowd as if to say, 'What do you ignorant peasants know of God?' And the Boss is looking at the Robed Ones and he's got that half-smile on his face. And maybe he's thinking, 'These people you so despise know more of God than you will ever know.'

And I like to think those peasants are a bit like the sparrows: not very dressy, but they know where it's at. No wonder he said 'Blessed are the poor.'

Personally, I would have preferred him to say 'Blessed are the sparrows.' But maybe that's what he meant as well.

And suddenly I realize he is watching me perched in this tree at the roadside and I have the strange feeling he knows what I am thinking.

Now the old men in their fine robes are moving away and the Boss has escaped the ambush. But he knows what they are thinking and he knows they will be back. And one day they are going to get him.

The real story

It's strange but, despite all the suffering brought on by the Occupation, there is still a lot of laughter to be heard in these parts. And the Boss can be the biggest joker around when he is in the mood. For example, nobody is likely to forget the day two of the Robed Ones showed up at the café in the market place where the Boss is having a coffee and a chat with some real rough customers from the city.

The Robed Ones have been sitting across the café at another table watching what is going on. Finally they must think they have seen enough for they walk across like a couple of policemen about to make an arrest and say to the Boss:

'Why do you do this? Why do you welcome to your table sinners and crooks and prostitutes like these people here, and eat and drink with them? You are a religious man and you must know that these people are nothing but scum and it is not right that you should befriend them in this way.'

At the mention of the word 'scum', one of the party reaches swiftly inside his coat in the manner of a person who might be carrying a gun; but the Boss holds up his hand as if to dissuade him.

'A religious man?' he says to the Robed One who has almost got himself shot. 'Well that is an interesting thought. But let us not dwell on that right now. You ask me why I welcome these people here and I will tell you. I thought we were commanded by God to love our neighbour as we are loved by God himself. And so that there is no misunderstanding, let me tell you a story about the love of God.'

He pauses for a moment and then, with a big grin, he says, 'In fact, we will all tell you a story.'

He turns and whispers something to several of the gang; and then he begins:

'Once there was a farmer who had . . .'

'Two sons,' says Andy.

'OK,' says the Boss, 'two sons. And?'

'And the younger son says to his father,' chips in Mary the Mags.

'I want my share of the estate. Now,' says Andy.

'And?'

One by one the others join in with the storytelling, which gets faster and faster.

'And the father says, "You must be joking. If I do that we will go bankrupt and how will we manage to run the farm with you gone? Not to mention what your mother will say if you suddenly move out." '

'Hmm . . .' says the Boss with a frown.

'OK, maybe the father says to the son: "This will be a terrible blow and we will all miss you. But I will do as you ask." And he gives the younger son his share of the inheritance.'

'And?'

'And the younger son takes off.'

'And?'

'Goes to live in a foreign country.'

'Where?'

'Where what?'

'Where what happens?' asks the Boss.

'Where he buys a flash car and spends his money in riotous living with gambling and prostitutes.'

'Prostituted women,' cuts in the Mags.

'What?'

'Prostituted women. Women don't get involved in prostitution unless they are forced to by men. Women who live in poverty.'

'You can't say that,' says Andy.

'Why not? It's true.'

'Well, it may be, but it spoils the flow of the story.'

'Tough,' snaps the Mags.

'OK,' says the Boss, 'He spends all his money in wild living. And?'

'And so he has to get a job.'

'But?'

'But jobs are hard to get because there is a recession. No – there is a famine.'

'And so?'

'And so he ends up hiring himself out as a labourer on a farm where he is made to look after the pigs,' says the Rox.

'Pigs?'

'Yes, filthy pigs,' insists the Rox beginning to enjoy the game.

'Then?'

'Suddenly one day he comes to his senses,' says Andy.

'Unusual for a man,' says the Mags.

Andy struggles on: 'And thinks to himself: the labourers on my father's farm eat better than this. I will go back to my father and I will say . . .'

Suddenly one of the Robed Ones leaps to his feet and roars in a deep voice: 'I have sinned.'

There is a stunned silence.

'What?' says the Rox.

'I said: "I have sinned." It's what the young son says next.'

'Who the hell gave you permission to join in our game?' says the Mags angrily.

'Hey, wait a minute,' says the Boss, 'anyone can join in our game.'

'Thank you,' says the Robed One. 'He says: "I have sinned and am no more worthy to be called your son. I have broken the law and I deserve to be stoned to death as prescribed in the law."'

'He says all that?' says the Boss. 'OK. And then what?'

'And then he goes back home,' says Andy.

'But?'

'But when he is still a long way off, his father sees him.'

'And?'

'Goes and gets his gun?' suggests the Rox.

'Not sure about that,' says the Boss thoughtfully.

'Goes to meet him and . . .'

'Suddenly all his pent-up anger is released in a torrent of rage and he curses his son who has brought disgrace on the family and on the community . . .' says the Robed One.

'He beats him up? Sends him packing?' suggests Andy helpfully.

'That's not quite what I had in mind,' says the Boss. 'More like: when the father sees him he runs to meet him. And before the son can say a word he throws his arms round him and kisses him.'

At this there is a chorus of disapproval.

'I don't think so,' says the Rox. 'No father would be so undignified as to run. And he is certainly not going to welcome the little weasel with open arms.'

'And the selfish boy hasn't made his apology to his father yet,' says the Robed One indignantly. 'For all the father knows, he could have come back to ask for more money. And in any case he is defiled with the filth of the pigs.'

'Trust me,' says the Boss grinning. 'The father does run down the lane and throws his arms round the filthy son and kisses him. And then he turns to the servants who have followed him and tells them: "Get my best robe and put it on him and a ring on his finger. Get shoes for his feet. For this boy of mine was dead and now he is alive. He was lost and now he is found. We will have a great celebration." '

'But that ruins the whole story,' says the Rox.

'But that is the story of the Father. It is the truth.'

'You are saying that is how God is?' says the Robed One. 'He welcomes people like that? People like these?' he says looking round the table in disbelief. 'With no apology or remorse? Without conditions?'

'Want a coffee?' asks the Boss. 'I think your friend has gone but you're welcome to stay.'

Over coffee the Robed One says: 'I think maybe you need to do a bit more work on the details, but you are right about the main thing. To love God and to love our neighbour is more than all the rest of the law put together. And I really enjoyed being part of your story.'

The Boss gives him a long look and says: 'You are beginning to catch on.'

But the Mags isn't quite finished with their unexpected guest. She says to the Robed One: 'You know earlier when you said the Boss was a religious man?'

'Yes.'

'Well, I'm not sure he is. Doesn't the word "religious" mean being tied? To a set of beliefs or a code or dogma?'

'Yes,' says the Robed One cautiously.

'Well, I don't think the Boss is like that at all. He's about setting people free. Untying them. Letting them go. Without conditions. That's what love's about isn't it?'

'So he's a man of God who isn't religious?' says the Robed One.

'Person of God,' says the Mags.

Seeing things his way

If I was to say the Boss is a bit bird-brained, you might think that I was lacking respect. Nevertheless I still say he is a bird-brain: and I am glad this is so, and I think that maybe God means him to be that way.

But the fact that many people might find such a statement insulting says a lot about how they think of birds – and other creatures, come to that. For how often do you hear some depraved or violent person referred to as nothing more than an animal? While people who are not very intelligent are called bird-brains.

So you really think depraved and violent people are animals? Well, if animals are so violent and depraved, then how come they do not fight wars and manufacture bombs and poisoned gas? How come animals do not keep each other locked up in internment camps and torture each other with electric wires and other terrible things?

Do they have gold-plated nests and burrows and other places where they hang out? Do they have slaves to keep them in luxury and make people work in oppressive conditions until they drop dead – just to make products very cheaply for the rich to buy one day and throw away the next? And this happens so much that the rich and powerful call this behaviour the free market, when really it is madness and greed. About which it is not wise to speak, unless you want to make some people very angry.

But, unfortunately, the Boss does speak about this. In fact he speaks a lot about money and the madness that it brings. And he makes people angry. Even some of the gang get hacked off with the things he says – especially Jude, who is one of his best buddies and who is called the Iscari. He is named the Iscari after the family he comes from who are very rich and we think this is what makes him so angry when the Boss talks about the money madness.

One day the Iscari is going on about how the gang need to have some money behind them to pay for proper accommodation and some decent clothes so that people will listen to them with respect. This is on account of how people always listen to people who wear good clothes and nobody listens to the bums who go round looking like they do not have any dignity.

But the Boss is very unhappy with this sort of talk for, indeed, he is always dressed like a tramp and most of his friends seem to be tramps and drop-outs and other people for whom the rich and powerful have no respect. And the Boss insists that God actually has a great care and respect for such people; and in fact it is the people with two cars and a swimming pool and bathrooms with gold taps that are deeply distressing to him.

And that is just where the argument starts, with the Iscari trying to get the Boss to see reason and get organized and do some fundraising and have some offices and resources; so that people will take him seriously – and maybe he should even stand for Mayor.

But the Boss is not having any of this and says that there is no way rich people will be able to get into the Kingdom of Heaven, whatever that means. Indeed, he says it is harder for the rich to get to this Kingdom than for a camel to get up a flea's backside; although I am not sure he uses exactly those words. But it is clear that this is what he means. Personally I believe the rich are so greasy that they will manage to get almost anywhere that will give them a profit on their investment.

But then the Boss hits the poor old Iscari with a sledgehammer. Jude, my friend, he says very quietly, you cannot be committed both to God and to Mammon. It is time to decide. It is one or the other. It is make-up-your-mind time.

'Oh, come on,' says the Iscari. 'You cannot be serious. Money is what makes the world go round and we have to live in the real world.'

But the Boss tells him that, while he loves him like a brother, the worship of money and the madness it brings is crucifying half the people on the planet so that tens of thousands of people are dying every day for want of clean water and food.

And the Iscari, who never knows when to shut up, says OK; so some people do get a raw deal, but the money the rich make gradually improves things for everyone. But even a blind dog with a deaf aid can tell you this is baloney since, from what I can see, the money madness only makes the rich more greedy while the poor get poorer.

But then the Boss comes out with something so completely crazy that the rest of the gang, who cannot help but hear what is going on between him and the Iscari, begin to feel a bit embarrassed, for the Boss says:

'You know who these people are who are dying of hunger because of the money madness? I am those people.'

Him? How can these people be him? Has the Boss gone crazy?

Maybe crazy. Definitely angry.

'I am the hungry one you force into starvation,' he says. 'I am the homeless one you uproot from the land. I am the one who dares to speak out in protest, who you throw into prison to shut me up. I am the one standing naked in the cold while your rich friends live in comfort. I am the one asking for justice – the one your newspapers call a parasite and a trouble-maker.'

Jude looks at him as though he is mad and says: 'When? When were you hungry or naked or cold? When were you in prison for asking for justice? What the hell are you talking about?'

And the Boss says: 'Make no mistake: when you did these things to one of these vulnerable ones, you did it to me. And if you did it to me, you did it to the one who sent me.'

At this the Iscari turns away, deeply distressed at what the Boss has said to him and, as he does so, he catches the eye of the gang who are watching what has been going on.

'Something's got to be done,' he says. 'We've got to bring him to his senses.'

But none of the gang knows what to say – or what to do.

And suddenly I realize the Boss has got a brain like a bird. He is seeing things as though he is high up in the sky so that, when you look down, people all seem pretty equal and there are no boundaries, and money does not matter so much. You realize what a beautiful place the world is, and how much God must love it to have made it so good.

And how grieved God must be at what is happening down there when people catch the money madness. And how much like a sparrow the Boss is: small and vulnerable, and not very well dressed. And I don't know why he doesn't just fly away and leave them to it. But he doesn't and it's as though staying around and taking the consequences is part of the love of God he keeps telling people about.

So it is no wonder the Iscari is saying that this can't go on and something has to be done to get him to change his attitude. There's got to be compromise, Jude is always saying. Know how to play the game. Because if you don't play by the rules you're going to get hurt.

But the Boss says something about only God rules. And everybody laughs. But the Iscari doesn't think this is very funny, because he is a realist.

And maybe, in his own way, he is only trying to protect the Boss.

The night of the great wings

There were few things more calculated to annoy my father. We never knew the reason: maybe it was because it was my mother's story and not his, that he could never enjoy it. Maybe because he did not understand it – and it was hard to understand. Perhaps because it was a mystery, and he did not like unfamiliar things.

Years ago he had stowed away – or fallen asleep – on a troop ship docked at a place called Tilbury. When he woke up they were far out to sea; too far to even think of flying back. A real cockney sparrow, he was horrified to discover he was on his way to some foreign place where a war was being fought. But, as they sailed along the coast of North Africa and the sun got warmer, his resolve to return home on the next ship began to weaken.

A week after they docked he met my mother, a golden-grey rock sparrow from the desert. And it was from the desert that the mysterious story came.

'Tell us the story, tell us the story,' we would say. And sometimes she would. And my father would groan and say: 'Not again,' and fly off into the night. Then my mother would open her wings, as if to hush the world, and very quietly begin to tell us again the Story of the Great Wings as it had been told to her – passed on down the generations.

One winter's night long ago, something amazing happened. Out on the hills at the edge of the desert an untidy convoy of travellers had pitched camp. Three rusted pick-up trucks, an ancient bus with boarded-up windows, and four old caravans: all drawn up round an open fire.

In the darkness beyond the firelight a small boy was guarding a flock of goats which grazed on the rough desert scrub. A woman was preparing food and a group of men, warming themselves by the fire, smoked their cigarettes and argued about their plans for the following day. Unnoticed, a small bird foraged in the grey sand for scraps of food.

Suddenly, no one quite knew how it began, there was a sound like the roar of a thousand motor-bikes. It started quietly but got louder and louder until the travellers by the fire, and the goats and the boy and the sparrow, were deafened by the sound of the approaching engines. They stood rooted like statues, unable to move. They realized they were going to die and a great fear came over them.

Then, beyond the hills, it started to get light as a golden glow turned the rocks and the sand from deep purple to red, through orange, to a whiteness so intense they could hardly bear to look. The intensity of the light continued to increase with the sound until their eyes and ears seemed to be bursting. At first some of them thought it was a nuclear attack and waited for the blast wave to tear their bodies to atoms, hurling them across the desert wastes into oblivion.

But as the sound and the light intensified to an unbearable brightness, it seemed they were being caught up, not in a final act of destruction, but in a colossal outpouring of power. And at the heart of that power there was something else. Music.

Then, quite suddenly, the deafening sound stopped and there was silence. And in the silence, shapes that stretched across the sky. Shapes that were moving and yet were still. Shapes of great wings that held back the night like an awning and revealed a world of light and colour and energy that seemed to go on and on for ever.

There was a rumbling that shook the ground. Then a voice, if it was a voice, for there was no sound, spoke. In their heads, men, women, boy, goats, bird – they all heard it, or thought they heard it. A birth, a child, a king, a leader, a servant, a danger, a hope, a sign, a beginning, a death, a gift, a challenge, a calling.

Go.

The music began again, but this time even louder; until they shook from fear and excitement, thinking they would die of shock, pulverized by the overwhelming force that engulfed them.

Then, in an instant, silence and the old familiar darkness. The goats continued to graze in the scrub but the others, men, women, boy and bird, stood still; frozen into disbelief at what had happened – or what they had dreamed.

They looked at each other, unable to put into words what they had seen. Then, like statues waking from an ancient sleep, they began to move; stumbling, staggering, circling each other. None of them daring to speak.

Finally, still without a word, like birds that sense a common direction, they set out for the nearby town leaving caravan, car and goat behind them in the darkness.

As they walked the streets, the small bird flying on ahead, the noise and bustle of the town brought them back to their senses. Each person they encountered was asked the same question: 'A birth? Tonight?' But people looked at them uncomprehending and turned away.

Finally, entering a crowded tavern to rest and think, they asked again: 'A birth? Tonight?'

'Round the back,' they were told. 'In the shed.'

Leaving their drinks untouched they hurried out into the street and down a dark, litter-strewn alley till they found the shed. Derelict and near to collapse, its door hung crookedly from rusted hinges.

Inside it was dark and cold. Dimly they made out the shapes of broken packing cases and empty oil drums. Finally they came to it. There was blood on the floor and, wrapped in rags, the child.

All this was long ago. So why am I telling it now? What does it matter? Maybe because of the mother. And the fact that today we are in the small hill town where it began, all those years ago.

She set off early this morning to try to find the place. It seemed important to her to return to where it all started. A birth that could so easily have been a death. And words someone had spoken: about those living in a land of deep darkness seeing in this child a great light.

It was late afternoon when she got back. I do not know whether she looked happy or sad but she had found neither tavern nor shed;

for they were not there. Instead, in their place, runs a concrete barrier erected by the army of occupation. Maybe she is relieved it is gone. It is not always wise to go back.

Later she talked about the birth. Why were they there at all? Identity cards. The card that gets you through the army checkpoints. All the people have to carry them and to apply you must return to the place of your birth so they know who you are. And if some people are too poor or too sick to make the journey, what does it matter? People without a pass shall not pass. Instead you stay where you are, unable to move. Imprisoned. An under-class. Non-existent.

Thirty years later and still the people are imprisoned. 'This is not how it is meant to be,' says the woman. 'Before he was born, I saw the great wings and a voice that told me of his birth. And in my head rang the words of Hannah's song: that the poor shall be raised up and the mighty put down from their arrogance.

'The hungry fed with the best of food; and the rich sent away empty. The love and justice of God will fill the world as was promised to those who have gone before us. And the child shall be called by a name that means God with us.

'But there was also a warning. Of hope – but also of pain and suffering.

'He is my son,' she says. 'My body and my blood.'

As she speaks it seems the story my mother told us of the night of the great wings may not be so crazy after all.

But later I get to thinking: why should such an amazing thing be shown to such people? Gypsies, shepherds, vagrants. And a sparrow. So that they become the ones who then go and tell what they have seen – they become the messengers.

The wise woman

It is generally reckoned that the Boss knows more about God than any man who ever lived. But not necessarily more than every woman.

The reason I have arrived at this unexpected conclusion comes about as a result of an encounter he has with a rather strange lady. Where she comes from, I do not recall. Some country whose name I cannot remember, and in any case, it does not matter what it is called.

It is a bright spring morning and we are out in the border territories, quite near to one of the military checkpoints, when this chance encounter takes place. Whether she has managed to get through the army roadblock without a pass, we do not know. Maybe she has done what many desperate people do, which is to avoid the checkpoints altogether by taking a long detour through the hills.

This is possible in the summer months but in the winter, when the ground turns to mud with the rains and there are often snow storms on the high ground, it is hard going. And there is always the chance of getting shot by an army patrol.

So there we are, minding our own business when suddenly, out of nowhere, this woman is standing in the road right in front of the Boss. No one has noticed her before but everyone can see by her clothes that she is a foreigner and there is slight unease because the country she is from is not a friendly nation.

In the past, before the army of occupation takes over, there are many border skirmishes and disputes, and the people of the one country do not even speak to the people of the other.

So it is a great surprise when the woman says to the Boss: 'Sir, I need you to come and fix my daughter who is very ill and I hear that you can do things for people like her. So please come and make her well again.'

But the Boss is not in such a compliant mood by the look of things, and he says in a very cheeky manner: 'Am I sent to your people? A people who are always making trouble and causing the argy-bargy and who are thinking they are better than everyone else? So how come you are suddenly asking me, a lowly foreigner, to help you?'

But the woman is not the least put off by what the Boss is saying and she replies in a very feisty way: 'Listen, wise-guy, all the time you are going around fixing people and giving them hope and respect and a vision of a new future, do you ever check their identity cards?

'I'll bet you never once ask where they come from or whether they are foreigners. In fact I do not think you have the word "foreigner" in your head, since you seem to be saying that we are all sisters and brothers. And if that is true, then none of us is foreign. So what is the big problem?'

The Boss opens his mouth to reply, but the woman is not done with him yet.

'Even if I am a foreigner and you are not sent to our people, you can still do this thing,' she says. 'Does not that sparrow which is always hanging around with you pick up the crumbs that drop from the table where you and your gang are eating? So cannot my daughter have the crumbs of your mercy?'

At this the Boss is about to say how they are all very respectful of the sparrow and put food to one side on the table specially for it to eat and do not expect it to peck around on the ground for crumbs which fall into the dust.

But then he realizes this will not help his argument, which he has now completely lost track of, due to the fact that the foreign woman seems to be talking a lot of sense. And in any case he is getting the strange feeling he has seen her before, though he cannot remember when.

Realizing he is completely defeated in his argument, which he was not very keen on winning anyway, he says: 'OK. I surrender. Let your daughter be healed.'

'I know my daughter is healed,' says the foreign woman.

'So?' says the Boss in some surprise, since he does not understand how she can know her daughter is healed.

'So, this is about you.'

'What about me?' says the Boss.

'Oh, maybe broadening horizons a little,' she says with a smile.

'Who are you?' says the Boss, suddenly getting the feeling he is not completely in control of things.

'My name is Sophie,' she says. 'Sophia, if you want to be formal.'

'And how do you know about us – and about the sparrow?'

'I know a lot about you.'

Then, before anything more can be said, she gives the Boss a light kiss on the cheek and walks away. In a moment she is gone.

'Who the hell was that?' says the Rox as if waking from a dream.

'She is Sophia,' says the Boss.

'It means wisdom,' says the Mags, looking thoughtfully down the road where the foreign lady has gone.

'Weird name for a woman,' says the Rox.

'You have a problem with that?' challenges the Mags.

'With what?'

'Women and wisdom. Or do you think wisdom is just a male thing?'

'Well, there have been wise men,' says the Rox.

'And there have been a hell of a lot of wise women. It's just that people don't often take the trouble to listen to them,' snaps the Mags.

Suddenly the Boss interrupts: 'Rox. You are not going to win this. Let us all go and have a coffee.'

Later, as they are sitting sipping thick black coffee, young John leans over.

'I've seen that woman before,' he says. 'I've spoken to her. She was hanging around a couple of months ago.'

'I know,' says the Boss, 'I saw her too.'

'Do you know her?'

'I think she's sort of a friend of a friend.'

'And do you think she was right? About broadening horizons?'

The Boss looks at him with a smile: 'I think that lady is right about most things.'

The thief in the night

Today the Boss is not looking too good. For a start it seems he has not got much sleep, on account of some strange visitor with whom he sits up talking half the night. And, for a second thing, there is a nasty rumour going round he may be implicated in a robbery.

Even the suggestion that the Boss may be linked with some act of stealing is a total nonsense, of course, since there is no more honest guy in all the world than him. On the other hand, there are rumours. And the fuss starts the moment it is getting light.

In this neighbourhood there are many poor people and some sleep rough on the streets, or hide themselves away in bombed-out buildings or even in rubbish skips that are left parked around the place.

One such person who is sleeping rough all the time in these parts is old Amos. Unlike many of the vagrants who roam the countryside, Amos is tolerated in this neighbourhood, partly on account of him being born in the area, and partly because he is blind. It seems the blindness comes upon him very suddenly many years ago in a tragedy in which his wife and three children are killed. After that he starts to hit the bottle and gradually loses everything he has.

And so it is that these days he is reduced to sleeping rough on the streets and has nothing to his name except an old grey blanket someone gives him and a pair of worn shoes that have holes so big that people sometimes wonder why he wears them at all. Although they admit it would be very degrading to have to walk round in bare feet, and so his worn-out shoes are somehow a part of his dignity.

Except that this morning all hell is breaking loose because old Amos has lost his shoes. Each night when he wraps himself up in his blanket to sleep he takes his shoes off; just like he did when he lived in a house with his wife and his children and was happy. Also he likes his feet to get some fresh air; it not being good for you if you wear the same shoes all the time, morning and night. And anyway no one will steal a pair of shoes that are so worn through like his are.

But during the night it turns out that this is exactly what does happen. As the old guy sleeps and dreams maybe of being able to see and of being with his wife and children again, a thief creeps up and steals his worn-out, busted-up shoes. So when old Amos wakes up and feels around for his shoes like he always does, he is greatly distressed to find them gone.

But there is even greater shouting and hollering when it turns out that a woman who is living across the road sees what happens. As she is getting up to light the fire for the day she sees, in the half-light of dawn, a figure coming out of a house and walking down the street.

Normally this would not be any big deal, except that this guy is robed in black with a hood pulled over his head like he does not want anybody to recognize him. The woman watches him closely because it is highly unusual for any of the Robed Ones to be up this early, since they are known to have a great liking for the easy life.

As she watches the figure in black, she sees him walk past the sleeping Amos who is curled up in his blanket in a doorway. But the man in black suddenly stops, as if a thought has struck him. Turning, he walks back very quietly and picks up the old guy's shoes. He looks them over carefully: then, to her amazement, he shoves the shoes under his robes and hurries off.

Later, when they ask her why she does not come out and tell the guy very sternly to give back the shoes to old Amos, she says she is afraid of the Robed Ones and does not want the secret police or the soldiers to be coming to her house in the night and maybe arresting people who do not know when to keep their mouths shut.

But what she does say is that the house this guy in black comes out of is none other than the house where the Boss is staying and, since no one in this neighbourhood knows anything about the Boss, there is much talk of how maybe they are in this stealing thing together.

So, all in all, the day is not getting off to a good start.

After a second cup of coffee, the Boss is now beginning to wake up and says he is not engaged in a life of crime, although it is true some of his best friends are generally regarded as the scum of the earth. However, he does admit that, during the night, something very strange happens.

A little after two in the morning he suddenly wakes up. Someone is at the door wanting to talk to him. At first he thinks this is some sort of trap, especially when it turns out that the visitor is one of the Robed Ones. But the visitor is not trying to trap him: in fact the guy seems pretty scared in case anyone should find out he has come to see the Boss.

At this, the Rox and Andy and several others chime in with the view that they also are feeling pretty nervous right now when they discover that, while they are asleep, the Boss is downstairs in the kitchen drinking coffee with one of the Robed Ones.

And what is to stop this spook going off and calling up the police and having them all arrested? And why the hell is he showing up in the middle of the night anyway?

But the Boss points out that the Robed Ones can call the police at any time of the day or night and have them all shoved in the slammer; so what does it matter whether the guy in black comes in the middle of the night – unless it is he who is the one scared of being found out.

'So what is this important thing he comes for, anyway?' demands the Mags, who is also very nervous about uninvited guests.

The Boss says this is a very good question, but he does not know the answer on account of how the visitor is reluctant to come out into the open with the reason for showing up so unexpectedly.

'So what does he say?' demands the Mags, getting exasperated.

'He tells me he thinks I am the one sent by God because of the things that happen when I am around, which he says could not happen unless God is in it. But I see he is struggling with something big on his mind like he wants to give up the old ways, so I try to help him.

'I tell him there is no way he can see the Kingdom of God unless he is born again.

'But he says: "How can I be born again when I am a grown man? Am I going to go back into the womb of my mother and be born a second time?"

'We talk for a long while and it is clear the guy is really trying to figure out what the Kingdom is all about and what it means for him.

'Finally he says "Maybe I am beginning to see the light." And I tell him I think maybe he is.'

'What happens then?' demands the Mags.

'I make him another cup of coffee and then he goes,' says the Boss.

'Yeah,' says the Rox. 'The man who does what is true comes to the light. Then he goes and pinches some old guy's shoes while he sleeps. Wonderful.'

Meanwhile, outside in the street there is a big commotion starting up and a young kid suddenly bursts into the room saying that the thief who came in the night and steals the shoes from old Amos has been back again.

Everybody piles out into the street and, sure enough, there is a big crowd gathered and people are shouting that they are going to find this guy with the black robes and beat the hell out of him, whether or not he is an important person and will send the gendarmes to come and arrest everybody.

The only person who does not seem to be shouting is old Amos who is sitting where he always sits when he is begging. But instead of calling to people to spare him a few coins, he is sitting in silence. He is holding a pair of shoes which some person has quietly put down on the blanket Amos spreads out to catch the coins people throw.

And Amos is silent because the shoes feel like his own shoes and they fit like his own shoes, but they have new laces in them. And the soles, which were worn through so bad no one knew why he bothered wearing them, have been mended so when Amos holds the shoes to his face he can smell the new leather. And he is gently running his fingers over the thick leather soles and feeling the strong new stitching, and in his head it is as though there is light in the darkness.

But they never do find out who has done this truly wonderful thing and the Boss says he cannot help them, for he does not know anything about a thief who comes in the night.

The elephant man

One of the saddest moments for the Boss comes the day he tries to make a miracle happen – and fails.

It all starts on one of the hottest days of the year. The Boss has been up since dawn and the early morning sees great crowds gathering to hear him speak. They like the way he talks because, nearly always, he tells them stories.

At first these sound like nicely-nicely stories, but at the end there comes a kick in the pants that really makes you think. Some people say the Boss should issue a health warning as some of these stories can seriously bump up your blood pressure.

Right now there is quite a bit of laughter going on for the crowds have gone and the gang are cooling off in the noon-day shade having a beer or two. The laugh is that Jez tells a simple little story this morning that makes the Robed Ones so mad they look like they are going to explode.

'Here,' says the Boss. 'The love of God for the lost: what is it like? I'll tell you what it is like. It is like a woman who loses a silver coin in the house. She searches high and low until at last she finds it. "Hey," she says to her neighbours, "I have found the coin that was lost, so come and celebrate with me." '

Which everybody thinks is a charming little story with a happy ending. Until the Robed Ones suddenly realize that the housewife in the story is God. When all the time they know that God is a man. So why does the Boss deliberately portray him as a woman?

Sitting in the shade, the gang ask the Boss to tell them another story, but the Boss says his throat is dry and he needs another beer. So why don't one of them tell a story for a change and give him a break?

But at this there is a great shuffling of feet because no one feels confident enough to tell a story, even if they had one to tell.

Fortunately, just at that moment, a car slows up and stops. And so does the conversation, for this is a very fancy car with an open top and in it are a young guy in an open-neck shirt and one of the most glamorous ladies the gang have ever seen, other than in the fashion magazines. Which is maybe where they do indeed see her. So the guy and the hot potato come and sit nice and quiet at a table on the edge of the group and order up a couple of chilled beers.

Then, to everyone's surprise, Andy suddenly announces: 'OK. I will do it. I will tell you a story, even though I am not very good at stories.

'This is a story you have never heard before because I made this one up myself and this is the first time I have ever told it to anyone.

'Once upon a time,' says Andy, 'there is this guy who is very rich. He lives in a big farmhouse, although he does not himself do the farming. He is too busy in the city making wagonloads of money from his business interests. He owns factories and casinos and properties, and who knows what else.

'And all the time this guy is getting richer and richer and stuffing his money into the bank and under his mattress and into pots and jars and even an old teapot in the kitchen cupboard. But the richer this guy gets, the more he craves for money. It is like he cannot bear other people to have money; he has to have it all.

'One day this guy has a most amazing idea. Very quietly he goes off into one of his barns and rolls the big doors shut behind him. Day after day there is the sound of hammering and the flickering blue light of a welding torch. As the weeks go by large crates are delivered to the barn; but no one knows what is going on inside.

'Finally, after many months have passed, the doors of the barn are rolled open and the people see the most astounding sight. There in front of them is a thirty-foot high metal elephant. And sitting on the back of this shiny metal elephant is the guy who loves money.'

By now the Rox is getting tired of listening to Andy, especially as many people seem to suddenly realize that Andy is more talented than they had thought. So the Rox says: 'This is a very stupid story since there are no elephants like this one you are speaking of; so can we all have another beer?'

But the rest of the gang tell the Rox to shut up and let Andy finish the story which they find very interesting, since even the Boss never tells them a story about an elephant.

So Andy goes on to say how the guy rides the metal elephant all over the town, and all over many other towns. And every time he comes to a house, the elephant sticks its long trunk like a vacuum cleaner down the chimney or in through a window and sucks up all the money there is in the house, until there is no money left: not even the silver coin that the housewife lost.

'And the greedy guy goes all over the place sucking up money from rich and poor alike. And every night he stuffs the money he has vacuumed up into the big barns that stand on his farmland until every one of the barns is bursting with cash . . .'

At this point Andy stops talking as though he is uncertain of what to say next.

'Well?' says the Rox. 'What happens after that? Why have you stopped before the story has ended?'

'I am very sorry,' says Andy, looking embarrassed. 'but I cannot finish the story, for I have not worked out how it ends. I did not know I was going to have to tell a story today.'

'How can you start a story when you do not know how it ends?' says the Rox in great disgust. 'That is a stupid thing to do and now we are stuck with a big metal elephant and loads of money and we do not know what to do with them. This is a real mess you have left us in.'

But then the Boss, whose throat has recovered a little with the cold beer, says: 'Maybe I will tell you how the story ends.

'The greedy guy with the elephant says to himself: my barns are so full of money that I cannot get another sixpence inside. So what shall I do? I will build some bigger barns so I can store up even more of the money. Then I can sit back and retire and never have to ride on this very uncomfortable elephant again. Then he goes to bed.

'But that very night, in his sleep, he dies.'

The Boss looks round at the gang: 'That is how it is with the guys who pile up treasures for themselves but who are paupers in the sight of God.'

'Well,' says the Rox, 'that is not a bad ending to the story. But it is all nonsense about a guy with a thirty-foot metal elephant that eats money. Whoever hears of such a thing?'

But just then there is a voice from a table on the edge of the group and the young guy with the posh car suddenly says: 'I am the elephant man.'

'What do you mean, you are the elephant man?' demands the Rox, annoyed that this stranger has interrupted him.

At this the young man walks over to the Boss and says: 'All my life I have been making money. All day I think of nothing else, even though I have more money than I know what to do with. And my Boss, Mr Mammon, is even worse than me, and I very much hope he does not hear this story about the elephant because he would certainly like to have such a method of sucking up money from the poor.

'But, in my heart, I know that this money is not good and that really my life is empty. What can I do? It is as though I am not alive.'

The Boss looks very kindly at the rich young guy and puts his arm round his shoulder:

'If you want to be alive,' he tells him, 'go and sell all that you have and give it to the poor.'

When he hears this, the rich young man is very alarmed because he has a heap of money and possessions, including the open-top tourer parked in the street.

'All of it?' he says. 'Everything?'

The Boss nods.

The young guy thinks this over for a few minutes. Then, looking so sad you think he is going to burst into tears, he says: 'I cannot do this.' And him and the nice-looking lady get into his fancy car and drive off.

The Boss is very quiet for a long time because it seems like he has taken a real shine to the young guy and is deeply sorry that he has walked away to an empty life filled with nothing but money.

'Cheer up,' says the Rox at last. 'Have another beer. It would have been truly a miracle if a guy like that had said yes.'

Die by the sword

Suddenly they are there like robbers that come silently in the darkness. Three cars pull up quietly outside. One minute everyone is asleep; the next moment, doors are smashed open. The sleepers are dazzled by the lights in their faces and guns are pressed to their heads.

'Not a word,' says one of them as they bundle the Boss out of the house and into one of the waiting cars. A blanket is thrown over his head and the car door slams.

There were seven, maybe eight of them – their faces covered. Who were they? The secret police? Special forces? Either way he is gone: their prisoner. The kidnap takes less than five minutes.

The cars drive quickly through the darkened streets and out into open country. No interrogation in the military compound – more likely a bullet in the back of the head and a shallow grave in the desert. Another of the thousands of disappeared. The tortured and abused. The imprisoned without trial. The executed. Rebels. Insurgents. Suspects. Fathers. Brothers. Sisters. Mothers. Children. All gone.

The speed of the kidnap leaves the gang shocked and confused: still half asleep. Outside, I take off after the cars, managing to keep up with them for a short time. But once out of town they drive fast and I lose them, their tail lights disappearing into the darkness.

No one sleeps the rest of the night. There is confusion and anger over what has happened. How it could have been prevented. Fear as to what will happen to the Boss. Whether they will see him alive again. The occupation forces are so powerful that no rescue is possible – even if they knew where he is being held.

Two of the gang – the ones the Boss calls the Sons of Thunder – are for going and getting guns for self-protection; others are in favour of staying put in the house. Some say they should split up in case the gunmen come back and more are arrested. The arguments go round and round till your head hurts. At last, unnoticed, there creeps in the first light of dawn. In the chill air faces are pale and drawn; ash trays full of cigarette butts and the table littered with empty coffee cups.

Then the sound of a car. A door opens and shuts. Moments later he is back with us: tired but smiling, as though something has amused him.

For a few minutes there is chaos with everyone yelling and talking at once. The Rox pushes through the scrum to hug him while young John sits on his own by the window in silence, close to tears. Finally Andy manages to bring the meeting to order:

'Are you OK?'

'I'm fine,' says the Boss.

'Where'd they take you?' cuts in the Rox.

'For a job interview.'

'Bollocks,' says the Rox angrily. 'Don't mess about. We were worried sick. Where did they take you?'

'I told you – for a job interview,' repeats the Boss with a grin.

Finally he has mercy on them.

It turns out this way: the kidnappers are rebels and they take the Boss off into the desert to a secret rendezvous. Here the Boss is greatly surprised to see many characters with guns – and among them several people you might read about in the newspapers and whom the military would pay big money to place handcuffs on.

At first the Boss thinks he is about to get the firing squad for things he has said in the past about love your enemy: an argument which does not find great favour among the militants.

But, instead of a last cigarette and an unmarked grave, the rebels explain to him that they have a problem. And he is the answer. Divided into different groups and factions, they do not have a leader who can unite them. They need someone who will be good on the TV and command international respect among decision makers. So they want the Boss to join them.

'Sure, the pay is not so good and there are no pension arrangements,' says one of them, 'but not everyone is invited to be a leading politician.'

Unfortunately, the Boss says he cannot do this even though it would be a great honour. And he keeps saying no, even when they suggest that an unmarked grave could be the alternative. But the Boss senses that they are not going to kill him: and they realize he is not going to change his mind.

So, finally, they have a few drinks and talk about this and that and the Boss tells them stuff about the Kingdom of God and these very serious people are greatly surprised to discover that even renegades like them who are fighting for a square deal for the poor may not be far from this Kingdom; whatever that is.

And the Boss tells them it may well be nearer than they think. Which often comes as a revelation to people who have been told all their lives that they are total zero and in all respects do not have worth and value – like the sparrows.

When Jez recounts these happenings to the gang, there is great consternation and debate. And the Monk, who is always looking for an excuse to pick up a gun, is somewhat disappointed at the outcome of the night's events.

He says turning down the rebels' offer was a dumb thing to do. 'We could have had some real muscle round here – maybe even with you leading an uprising.'

But the Boss is not impressed. 'Those who live by the gun will die by the gun,' he says.

'Weren't you even tempted to say yes?' asks the Rox. 'What about the power it would give us?'

For a moment the Boss frowns as though he has just remembered something bad. Something from a long time back. He doesn't say anything for a while. Then he tells them a story that scares everyone half to death.

In the early days when he is trying to figure out what God is asking of him, he takes off into the desert to think and to pray. After he has been out there for a long time the heat begins to get to him.

A fly is buzzing around, and by now he is starving. Suddenly he notices how the rocks look like loaves of bread. And how good it would be if he could change the rocks into bread and eat.

There is a moment's silence as the gang sense that something more important than bread is going on.

'And so did you?' asks Andy, breaking the silence.

'No,' says Jez. 'I remembered that thing about not living by bread alone but by every word that God speaks.'

'So then what?' says Andy.

The gang listen in silence as the Boss tells them how he is trying to get his thoughts straight about what he should do. It is as though the fly is tormenting him. Suddenly he starts hallucinating. He is up high on a mountain-top. All the countries of the world are spread out before him. And a voice is saying: you can be the ruler of all this if you pack in this God thing.

'And?' says Andy.

'I said: "God is all there is." '

'And last night it was happening again? The promise of power and all that?'

'That's right,' says Jez.

Everybody sits in silence thinking about what the Boss has said. And the Mags gets up and walks over and stands in front of him and presses his head into her breast and holds him for a long time. And the tears are running down her face and off her chin and dropping down onto the top of his head like they could wash away the pain.

Then John, who is over by the window, suddenly says: 'What did you say about bread?'

Everybody stares at him as though he is crazy, so that he turns away looking embarrassed. He has a bit of paper and a biro in his hand and it looks like he's been writing stuff down.

But who cares about that?

A leap in the dark

Some things are a complete mystery to me. For example: when old Amos gets his shoes fixed by the guy in the black robes, everybody expects him to be happy. But for some strange reason this is not so. Instead, day by day, he sinks deeper into despair.

How bad things are getting I see for myself one morning. Here I am resting on a window ledge waiting for the sun to rise and get everything warmed up. Below, in the first light of dawn, I can see Amos asleep under his old grey blanket – the only thing that keeps him from freezing to death when the nights turn cold.

For some time now the old guy has been tossing and turning and muttering in his dreams, which must be real bad ones the way he carries on. Underneath the blanket he is holding his newly repaired shoes. Every night he does this, holding tight in case they get stolen again. But, in his sleep, it seems the shoes remind him of something else: maybe a house where a sleeping child clutches a soft toy for comfort.

It is certainly as though the shoes stir deep memories of the past: memories best forgotten. Of times when he was alive and life was good.

Suddenly the old guy sits bolt upright with a cry of pain. A dog, which has been sleeping nearby, lifts its head and pads over to the man who is staring wildly like a corpse. The dog pushes its muzzle into the old man's face and licks away the tears.

Gradually the man wakes, pressing the dog's head against his chest with one hand; still clutching the shoes in the other. At last, with a deep sigh, he falls back on the ground and speaks quietly to the dog which lies down beside him.

Why the shoes should stir up so much pain, I do not know. Also, I am mystified as to why the Boss seems to be ignoring the blind beggar; which is a very unusual way for him to carry on, since he is normally very supportive of such people.

For several days now he and the rest of the gang have been staying in the town where the Boss has been talking to the people very powerfully about the love and justice of God and how he has been sent to bring them freedom from their oppression. And yet here is this old guy whose life has been destroyed by just such oppression, and the Boss does nothing. Even the gang have commented on this, especially the Mags, for they are all deeply concerned at the seeming indifference the Boss is showing.

Maybe, however, there is something else going on, for I get to thinking that the Boss is not ignoring the old guy so much as waiting. But waiting for what, I do not know. And all the time the blind beggar is sinking deeper into despair.

It is as though the mending of the shoes reminds him that he is a human being with value and dignity. For fixing shoes with real leather soles does not come cheap these days – and that seems to make things even worse. As though this act of kindness may be the death of him.

For it seems that, in his mind, long-buried memories are being awakened. The day the planes appear. Bombs falling out of a clear blue sky on shops and houses. The bodies of his wife and children. The open grave. And then dry earth and rocks quickly shovelled in, crushing the bodies of those he loves.

Later they find him lying beside the grave: eyes wide open to the blazing sun. He never saw again. Nor did he want to.

And still the Boss says nothing. In fact today things get even worse. The crowds are getting dangerously large and it is no longer safe to talk to them in the town. Informers may alert the soldiers to what is happening. Public meetings are banned these days for fear the rebels will stir up trouble. Instead, early in the day, the Boss sets off into the desert. Later, it is as though the town quietly empties as people slip silently away from shops and houses to find him.

By mid-day the place is deserted. At the side of the road sits old Amos, his blanket spread out to catch the coins that people throw. Except there are no people. Only the dog lying beside him in the heat.

For hours the old man sits in silence. Suddenly he stops stroking the dog's head and looks up as though someone has spoken to him. On his face there is a strange look. The dog watches him, unsure what is going on.

In the distance comes a growing murmur of voices as the crowd return. The Boss is speaking, but not everyone can hear and there is a gentle jostling to get closer to him.

Suddenly old Amos starts yelling: shouting to the Boss. The crowd, who are already having trouble hearing what the Boss is saying, naturally tell the old man to shut up. But, at this, the old guy shouts even louder:

'Son of David,' he yells. 'Son of David, have mercy on me.'

The crowd are now getting angry with the old guy — partly because he refuses to shut up when they tell him; and partly because the stuff he is shouting is very dangerous talk indeed. This 'son of David' thing is like a coded message. The words signify someone is a king or great leader. The crowd knows if word of this gets back to the authorities, there could be trouble.

Meanwhile the Boss has stopped and I can see he has that half-smile on his face. Maybe the thing he has been waiting for all this time has started to happen.

He tells the people to let the old man through. At this there is much grumbling from the crowd who reckon he deserves a good thrashing, even if he is blind.

But it looks like they will have the last laugh, for when the old man hears the Boss is calling to him he makes a big mistake. As he gets up he throws aside his blanket, leaving it lying in the road as he stumbles towards the Boss. In his blindness he does not know where it has gone, or whether someone has taken it.

In fact the blind beggar has forgotten all about the precious blanket. As he pushes through the crowd he is thinking only of one thing.

Finally, he stands before the Boss.

117

'What is it you want me to do?' says the Boss.

'He wants money,' yells someone in the crowd. 'They always want money.'

'He wants more beer,' shouts another.

'He wants teaching some bloody manners,' calls out someone else, and there is laughter.

The Boss is also smiling. But not at the crowd.

'What is it you want me to do for you?' he asks again.

For a moment the old man is silent. Then he reaches out until his fingers touch the Boss's shirt. Maybe he does want money, or a bed for the night. Maybe he just wants a beer to help deaden his pain.

As he stands, his hand against the Boss's chest, he can feel the heart beating. Then he takes the leap:

'I want my sight back,' he says.

There is laughter from the crowd. And still the Boss is smiling. Then he puts his hand on the old guy's shoulder, leaning forward so that only Amos can hear.

Suddenly the crowd is silent. Amos is looking at the Boss:

'You're younger than I thought you'd be,' he says.

The Boss smiles. 'It's time to go home,' he tells the old man.

But the old guy does not go home. Instead he strings along with the rest of us. Him and the dog. And everyone is glad the old guy can see once more.

But there will come a day when Amos wishes he was blind again.

The gift of life

The woman says nothing. When they bring home the body and peel away the remains of his clothing to wash him, she says nothing. Even when they lay him in the open coffin like he is sleeping, she does not speak. It is as though she is deaf to the grieving of her neighbours going on all round her. She is a widow and he was her only child and he is dead; but she says nothing.

They carry the coffin out of the curtained gloom of the small house into the dust of the street, and the glare and heat of the sun hits them like a blow. But her eyes are dry and unblinking, and still she says nothing.

They walk slowly along the torn-up street, stumbling over the rubble. In the crowd stand the two children who were with him, but they say nothing.

It was only yesterday that they were playing in the street when the tanks came and with them a machine they had never seen before. The tanks with their revolving turrets with the big guns were familiar. They also knew about the machine-guns the tanks have. But this strange machine is different. It looks like a bulldozer: but on the back is fixed a great steel hook.

The hook tears up the tarmac of the streets like a plough; ripping up telephone cables, water pipes, gas pipes and electric cables so the lights go out in the shops and houses and in the local hospital that is almost closed anyway because of the shelling. The children stand and watch the great steel hook ripping up the street as though they are in a dream. Then one of them, the boy, picks up a stone, like he has seen older boys do. He throws it at the strange machine.

The stone falls short because the boy is only seven years old and is not very good at throwing stones. Suddenly one of the tanks opens fire with its machine-gun and bullets come zipping down the street; but the two children do not know which way to run and they stand frozen with fear. And all the time the strange machine goes steadily along the street, ripping up the road, and the bullets are still coming down the street from one of the tanks.

People are shouting at the kids from the houses nearby, but the children do not move. Then a man breaks cover and runs, stooping low, as if to dodge the bullets. He runs at the kids like a rugby player, snatching them up, one under each arm, not breaking his stride as he reaches them.

He runs straight across the street and into an empty house. The machine-gun stops firing and there is a moment of quiet as the tank turret revolves like a great animal picking up the scent of its prey. The tank moves slowly back down the street. Then it fires a single round. The shell smashes a large hole in the concrete wall of the house. The explosion blows a sudden cloud of dust and debris out through the open doorway and broken windows.

Later, when the tanks and the strange machine with the great hook have gone, the people find them. The man is lying across the bodies of the little boy and the girl. Somehow the children are alive but the man, who is maybe in his early twenties, is dead.

When they finally come to examine his body they find no sign of injury. It is as though he has died of heart failure from compression from the shock of the shell exploding. They go and tell his family, but there is only his mother and she says nothing. After the rest of the family are killed she has no more tears to cry and no more words to speak. It is as though she knows before they tell her, that he is dead.

Now they are walking slowly along the ripped-up street. The tanks have driven over the pavements so the paving slabs are smashed up and there is no even ground to walk on. So, as they go, the coffin is jolted from side to side, which seems very disrespectful of the young man who died saving the two young children, who stand in silence and watch. But the mother who is walking behind the open coffin does not seem to notice this. Even in the white heat of the sun, her eyes do not blink and it is as though she too is dead.

120

About now the Boss and the gang are on the outskirts of the small town hoping to find food and water after their long march. Ahead they can see a commotion and the sound of shouting and crying carries through the still air. As the funeral procession approaches, the gang and the rest of the crowd move aside to let it pass. But the Boss stays standing in the middle of the road as if to block the way.

For a moment it looks like the people at the front of the funeral procession will push him aside, but instead they come to an uneasy halt. The Rox goes over to the Boss as if to pull him away from this embarrassing confrontation, but then he sees the Boss has that look on his face again: half sad, half smiling.

He walks forward through the leading mourners until he comes right up to the foot of the open coffin. For a while he just stands there looking across the body of the dead son into the face of the widow. But she says nothing, and it seems she does not even see the Boss is there or notice the procession has stopped.

The Boss touches the coffin, which is a very intrusive thing for a stranger to do, but she does not speak. Even when he takes the hand of the dead man, which is a deeply shocking thing to happen and is totally forbidden by the law, since touching a dead body means you are defiled: even then she says nothing.

And the Boss looks at the young man whose body was not marked by the shell that killed him. He says something which nobody can hear because there is so much shouting and anger because he has touched the body of the man who they loved. And then the guy in the coffin opens his eyes and looks at the Boss and gives him a slow smile, like they are friends from a long time back. And the widow says nothing. But there are warm tears falling down from her eyes into the coffin like gentle rain on the face of the boy who is her only child. And she is not dead after all.

And all hell is breaking loose in the crowd as many people are shouting and yelling and some people have keeled over with the shock. And one guy is so angry that he is jumping up and down, and it turns out he is the undertaker who has suddenly realized he may not be getting paid for his work. He wants to know what he is going to do with an empty grave it has taken him several hours to dig in the ground where there are many rocks and sometimes shells that come from the occupation forces which do not explode. Not until some kid picks one up out of curiosity.

But all is not lost, for it turns out that there is a funeral tea waiting to be eaten which seems very agreeable to the gang. And it seems OK also for the guy who was dead – even though, he admits, this is a very unusual situation.

Later, as they are all eating and drinking and a very lively party is in progress, the widow leans across the table and says to the Boss: 'Why are you here?' But whether she means 'Why are you here just at the moment when my only child is going to be buried' or whether she means something else, we do not know.

And the Boss thinks for a minute and then he says to her: 'Why am I here? I am here that you may have life.' He looks around at the party going on around them and says: 'Life like this: life in all its fullness.' And the woman whose son was dead says nothing. But she is smiling to herself.

'What are you thinking?' asks the Boss.

'I am thinking whether the life you speak of is just for me and my son who was dead. Or maybe whether it is life for all the world. I am thinking about who you are,' she says.

But the Boss says nothing.

The Boss gets a surprise

Despite the rough life, there weren't many times we got fed up. But once I remember Jez getting really low. We were sheltering in the ruins of some bombed-out village. The place was significant for two reasons. First, the brutality with which it was destroyed. Before the bombing began, more than two hundred villagers: men, women, children and the old were shot. A few others fled in terror, leaving their belongings behind them. Then came the bombs.

The second reason the village was important was that it served as a warning to other places the Army wanted to shut down. The domino effect. After reports of the first atrocity, other villages were swiftly abandoned without any resistance or a shot being fired. In all, more than four hundred villages were cleared, leaving strategically valuable land free for military use.

Although it was almost forty years since the killings, the ruined and deserted village still had a feeling of sorrow about it.

Maybe it was because it was a chilly night, or maybe the thought of all the people who had died was getting to the Boss. Suddenly he says something about: 'The birds of the air have their nests and the foxes have their holes, but the Son of Man has nowhere to lay his head.'

None of us was quite sure what this Son of Man stuff was about, but it was as if he was talking both about himself and about other people in the same situation. He could have been saying the poor have no place to rest their heads: who knows? It was as though he was feeling their pain. And maybe the pain the people of the village had suffered all those years before. And here we are camped out in the ruins of the houses that have been their homes.

It is cold. There is no food and no furniture; so there's nothing much to do except turn in for the night. The Boss is sitting in silence on the earth floor of the ruined house. Its windows are long since gone and the roof is open to the night sky.

The Mags sits looking at him across the fire: sad and thoughtful. After a while he realizes she is watching him.

'What?' he says.

'You.'

'Me what?'

'Resting your head.'

'Where?'

'Over here,' she says. 'Sit with me. Put your head in my lap.'

Nothing like this has happened before. Beautiful, even with her bashed-in nose, the Mags is a seriously tough lady. Not someone you expect to be warm and sensitive.

She holds out her hand. 'Come on.'

The Boss walks over and sits down with her on the blanket she has spread on the floor. Then she puts an arm round him and holds him very close. And it seems to me the boy's been needing some holding for a long time.

Then, very gently, she pulls him down so his head is resting in her lap, like a mother comforting a child.

They are still for a long time and I think they have gone to sleep in the firelight. But in the quietness of the night a thought has just come to the Boss.

'Mags,' he says.

'Go to sleep. Rest.'

'No, Mags. I need to ask you something.'

'In the morning.'

'No; now.'

'Well?'

'That time when they arrested you. You were angry with me.'

'That's right. Very angry.'

'With me?'

'With you.'

'But it wasn't me who was trying to have you executed. The men who caught you . . .'

'In the act of adultery?'

'That's right.'

'No. That's wrong.'

The Boss suddenly sits up.

'But you said . . .'

'No. If you remember, I didn't say anything. As I recall, you didn't even ask me whether I had anything to say before they started throwing rocks at me. It didn't seem to occur to you there might have been a different version of the story.'

'So what did happen?'

'Think back. I had a black eye, a bust nose and my clothes were torn. Had I been making love? No, you idiot. I was being raped. Except he didn't get what he wanted. I can be very determined.'

'So what happened?'

'When people heard the din and came to investigate, he started yelling that I was mad and cleared off. Then the Robed Ones suddenly realized they could use me to trap you, and they hauled me away.'

'But why didn't you say anything?'

'Nobody was listening. Certainly not the Robed Ones. They were too busy knocking me about. Anyway, you managed to turn the whole thing round so neatly I almost stopped being angry. Up to then I thought you were just another man, but that was cool. Though if someone had thrown that first stone I'm not sure I'd have been very amused.'

'So what about when I said "sin no more"?'

'Yes, I was pretty mad about that. But, later, I thought about how we've all done plenty of sinning; so that wasn't a problem. It's just that they weren't the sins you had in mind. As the days went by I got to thinking about the way my life was going – and I suppose I drifted back to see what else you were up to.'

'But you've never said anything about it since then. Why not?'

'I don't know. There never seemed a right time. Anyway, I quite enjoyed being one up on you.'

'So what happens now?'

'You lie down and stop talking.'

She pulls him down so his head is on her lap again and very gently strokes his hair; soothing him.

Somewhere far away in the darkness there is the sound of gunfire, or maybe it's just a car backfiring. The Boss is still half awake but he isn't listening to the noises in the night.

'Mags,' he says drowsily.

'What?'

'You're a good friend.'

'So are you,' says the Mags looking thoughtfully into the glowing embers of the fire. 'So are you.'

In the stillness she gazes up at the stars which seem to fill the night sky. One is much brighter than the rest. Maybe the Pole Star.

'You are our guiding star,' she says softly, still stroking his head. 'Always pointing us towards the love of God. No wonder you get lonely sometimes.'

But the Boss does not reply: he is fast asleep.

The Mags smiles to herself. There is no place she would rather be: but she knows things will not always be this peaceful.

When the bad times come

The forecast is not good. Often they get it wrong: but the storm warning is no mistake. Dark rain clouds have been gathering for days and now the air is still as we wait for the first crash of thunder. In the trees the birds are silent. The Boss is also silent. Not on account of the weather, but because he knows a more dangerous storm is brewing.

The gang can be unruly and wild but they are also vulnerable. The Rox is typical: big and honest, but liable to make mistakes. The Mags, bright and strong and with a lot of sense: but, like the Boss, unwilling to compromise. Young John, quiet, clever and so intuitive it is like he can read the Boss's mind. He senses trouble ahead but, like the Mags, is ready to confront it. James and the other John, the ones the Boss calls the Sons of Thunder, have no idea of what may be coming. The same goes for Andy and Tom and the Monk.

The Iscari seems to sense the danger but even he does not know how it will come about; although he may suddenly find he is the cause of it. And what about the strange foreign woman, Sophie, who has started showing up? Maybe she knows it all, as though she can see into the future. She is silent like the Boss. But while he seems uneasy, she is calm and watchful.

Finally, the Boss comes to a decision. He calls the gang together: the women, young John, the twelve and all the others. The Boss has something important to say, but his words are unlike anything they have heard before.

'Take care,' he says. 'Take care you are not misled. Many will come claiming my name and saying: "I am he." But do not follow them.

'When you hear of wars and uprisings, do not be afraid. These things are bound to happen. Nation will go to war against nation and kingdom against kingdom.'

The Boss speaks for a long time; the gang listening in uneasy silence. He warns them they will be arrested and put in jail; they will be betrayed by their friends – even by their relatives. 'Some of you will even be put to death,' he says.

'Be on the alert. Pray at all times for strength to pass through all that is coming. When this happens, stand upright and hold your heads high, because your liberation is near.

'And now,' he says, 'I will teach you the rest of the Great Prayer.'

Young John smiles: 'You mean the EWP?'

'The EWP?' says the Boss looking puzzled. 'What is that?'

'It is the Eight Word Prayer you taught us,' says young John. 'We do not think it is as long as the prayers other people say, but we know it is very deep. In fact I still have not finished praying these eight words: and to tell the truth, it takes me a long time to pray even this first word, Abba.'

At this there is a murmur of laughter and everyone is glad that young John makes a gentle joke that breaks the tension of what the Boss has been saying, although they know that the bad stuff has not gone away. Even so it is good to smile a little in the face of danger.

And the Boss is also laughing. 'OK,' he says. 'I will make this very simple for you. The first part of the Great Prayer is only three lines long, so you can remember it easily. And the last part of the prayer is also three lines long – for the same reason. Also,' he says, 'as times get tough you will definitely need to pray these last three lines if you are true to your calling.'

I see young John has a little notebook he bought a few days back and a biro. He is determined not to forget these words; for he knows they may be the most important he will ever hear.

Then the Boss begins: 'When you pray you should say: Abba, your name be hallowed. Your kingdom come. Give us today our daily bread. Forgive us our debts as we have forgiven those who are indebted to us. And do not bring us to the time of testing.'

After he finishes telling them the prayer there is silence because, although there are now three more lines and the prayer is double the length it was, it is still very short. And after the warning he has just given them, six short lines do not seem that much. Also, they are not quite sure what these new lines mean and there is much muttering.

Tom says he does not know why we are praying for bread because we have nowhere to keep the bread. And if we pray for bread each day, that seems to be a very doubtful way to carry on when you do not know where your next meal is coming from.

The Iscari says he thinks it is better if we pray for money so we can keep it in reserve and buy what we want, when we need it.

One of the women says we have to have faith and trust God and this is why we pray for bread only for today – or maybe it is for tomorrow, as she cannot remember the exact words the Boss has just told them. Meanwhile the Mags says it is like the prayer from the old days that talks of the hungry being filled with good things and the rich being sent away empty. But the Iscari says it is always the poor who go away empty and that is why we need money to make sure we are fed.

But then the whole thing is interrupted by young John who says something that absolutely nobody understands, for he suddenly says to the Boss: 'You are the bread.'

'What bread?' says someone.

'I don't know,' says young John. 'It just came into my head. Like he is our life and bread is life. Each day he gives us life. Like bread. Feeding us with the word of God. Almost like he is the word of God.'

'Never mind that,' says the Rox suddenly. 'What about this forgiving thing? Why should people cancel the debts that are owed to them?'

There is a murmur of agreement with this point of view. So the Boss does what he always does when he is trying to help the gang unscramble a puzzle: he tells them a story.

Once, he says, there was a servant who owes his master a huge amount of money. If he does not pay up he will be thrown into prison along with his wife and children.

But the master decides to have mercy on the servant and he announces that the debt is cancelled. Suddenly the servant is free and there is great rejoicing.

But no sooner does all this happen than the servant spots another servant who owes him a very small amount of money. And he grabs him by the throat and starts to throttle him and demands the money that is owing.

When he hears about this the master is furious and puts the ungrateful servant into prison after all, and throws away the key. Be merciful as your Father in heaven is merciful to you, says the Boss. Forgive and you will be forgiven and it will be given to you, in good measure, pressed down and running over.

Outside it is quite dark now and the Boss is getting worried the gang will forget the last line of the prayer which he says they must remember for, though it is the last line, it is still important.

When the bad times come, he says, they will be tempted to run away from the ordeal; tempted to despair; tempted to be led astray; and maybe even tempted to lose their trust in God. If you want to be true to God, he says, you have to be willing to leave your own self behind. Like I told some of you in the early days, you will need to take up your cross and follow me.

They are all quiet when they hear the word 'cross' because they are thinking what that terrible word means. It is silent in the room for a long time as though they are lost in their own thoughts.

The only sound is the buzzing of a fly which settles on the table close to the Boss's hand. Outside there is a rumble of thunder and we hear the first heavy spots of rain on the roof. And we know the bad times are coming.

Life and death

People are a complete mystery to me. They say life is important: some even say it is sacred. So why do so many of them go and put themselves in danger? And then everybody complains when things go wrong and they end up dead.

This life and death stuff suddenly arises one day when the Boss is away making arrangements for the next part of the journey. Meanwhile the gang and a few of the others are hanging about waiting for him to get back and Andy has picked up a newspaper.

'There is bad news in the papers today,' he announces. 'Two climbers are killed in a mountain accident and a load of people are dead from drowning on a beach somewhere.'

'How do you end up dead on a beach?' asks the Rox. 'Beaches seem to be pretty safe places, compared to being out in a fishing boat.'

'They went out on the mud-flats picking shell-fish and suddenly they were caught by the tide. The water comes up so fast they could not get back to dry land and many of them ended up being drowned. Maybe twenty or thirty of them are dead, although they haven't found all the bodies.'

'I do not know why God allows such things to happen,' says the Iscari. 'If he is a loving God, like the Boss says, then how can he let people die like this?'

'Maybe people should check the tide tables before they go out at low tide,' says the Rox. 'Tides have been coming in and going out every day for many years and people should have figured out that it will happen again the day they go on the beach. People should learn to treat the sea with respect.'

'So it is OK for forgetful people to get killed?' says the Iscari.

'No, it is not OK,' says Andy. 'But what do you want God to do: hold back the tide? Have steps and a hand-rail up every mountain? Drain the Atlantic every time some ship hits an ice-berg?'

'How are you going to be safe, anyway?' asks the Rox. 'Stay in bed wrapped in a duvet? Never let go of your mother's hand? You would go nuts. Maybe danger is the price we pay for freedom. It is definitely the price we pay for fish.'

It is so unusual for the Rox to say anything profound that, at this, there is a complete silence. No one seems to have noticed that the Boss has slipped quietly into the room.

But the Iscari cannot bear to lose an argument: 'All the ancient books tell the same story,' he says. 'God wants us to be safe and secure. Families living in harmony. Plenty of food and enough money to make sure we do not go hungry. Peace on earth. Isn't that right?' he says, turning to the Boss.

It is only now that people realize Jez has returned and, by the look on his face, things are not going so well.

'Security?' he says. 'Peace? I have told you before, I do not come to bring peace; I have come to bring life and freedom.' He pauses for a moment as if a thought has come to him: 'But whoever wants to save their life will lose it, and whoever risks their life will save it.'

'Yes, but we need to be prudent,' insists the Iscari. 'To be sensible and have money in reserve, surely? To build on the success we have achieved so far.'

'But what does it benefit you if you gain the whole world and forfeit your life?' snaps the Boss. 'Remember what I have told you: take heed and beware of all greed; for a person's life does not consist in the amount of their possessions.'

The gang are a bit taken aback by the tone of the Boss's voice, since the Iscari has only been saying what seems sensible.

But the Mags is picking up on something else.

'What are you saying?' she asks the Boss. 'What is this life that is forfeit? Who are you talking about? And, anyway, where have you been?'

He smiles and looks round the group. 'Let me ask you a question,' he says. 'Who do you say that I am?'

'What?' says the Mags. 'What do you mean, who are you?'

'Just what I said,' says the Boss. 'Who am I?'

For a moment there is complete silence. Then the Rox says: 'You are it. The Christ. You are the Son of God.'

Before anyone can say anything, the door suddenly bursts open and three men enter the room. In a moment everyone is on their feet ready for a fight.

'What are you looking for?' demands the Rox belligerently.

'Him,' says one of the men looking at the Boss. 'We are here to warn you. You must get away from here. They are coming to pick you up.'

'Who's coming?' demands the Rox.

'The District Administrator. He's sending soldiers. He wants you off his patch.'

'Go back and tell that old fox not to worry,' says the Boss. 'I have a few things to finish and then I must be on my way.'

'On your way where?' demands the Rox.

'South. To the city.'

'The city? But that's madness,' says the Rox. 'They'll be waiting for you: that's just what they've been hoping for. You cannot go there. I won't let you.'

The Rox seems almost in tears but his attempt to steer the Boss away from trouble just seems to make him angry and he suddenly turns on the Rox:

'Get out of my sight,' he says. 'You are like the enemy.' And then he adds very quietly: 'Like I said: he who would save his life will lose it.'

The atmosphere is pretty tense after that and people start to drift off as if they are too embarrassed to stay. The pressure seems to be getting to everybody.

Later Andy and the Mags are sitting in a corner of the room talking about the events of the evening.

'What the hell was all that about?' says Andy. 'The Rox was only trying to save the Boss's skin. Why should he get so angry about that?'

'Maybe because this is it,' says the Mags.

'What is it?'

'The end.'

'The end of what?'

'The end of everything.'

'What are you talking about?'

'You heard him. He has a few things to finish and then he's going to the city.'

'So?'

'You know what they call it in the old books: the city that murders prophets. Prophets: as in people who stand for justice; who speak the word of God – and get silenced by people who don't want to hear that word. By people who are in positions of power. People with vested interests. What was it he said: greedy people in love with their possessions.'

'They're going to kill him?'

'Maybe not, but they certainly need to shut him up. They don't give a damn about him healing people; what's making them really mad is that he's destroying their whole system. Giving bread to the hungry is one thing, but he's doing much more than that. He's giving them self-respect and hope and the vision of a new way to live. The poor shall be filled with good things and the rich sent away empty. The weak raised up and the powerful brought down. And why? Because that's what God says must happen. Dangerous stuff, Andy. So it would suit them just fine if he were to vanish into some prison camp far away in the desert.'

'But why go to the city? Why walk into a trap? What's the point?'

'Because the Rox is right. Crazy as it may sound, this guy is it. The Christ, or whatever you want to call it. The one who speaks the will and purpose of God. Is that person going to back off because a bunch of old men in black frocks want him out of their hair? This is the one who young John is saying is the word of God. Is that person going to let some tin-pot army stop him? No, Andy: he's going all the way. Because that's what the love of God means. To stop would be to deny that love.'

'How do you know all this?' says Andy.

'Intuition.'

'Are things going to get bad?'

'I think the tide's coming in,' says the Mags.

Demons in the head

She was probably the most beautiful girl they had ever seen. I say girl but maybe she was almost a woman; who am I to know these things? And what does it matter whether she was beautiful or not, except that it made the father's grief seem deeper than it might otherwise have been.

'She is my baby,' he tells the Boss, 'and she is going to die. One day soon I know she will be dead. She is fourteen and I love her. I need you to fix her so that she lives.'

'Is she sick?' says the Boss. 'She looks OK to me.'

'In her head she is sick,' says the father, almost in tears. 'In her head she has demons. They throw her to the ground unconscious; they throw her down as she crosses the road and she is almost killed by a truck. Then, another time, she is drying her hair in front of the electric fire and the demons throw her against the red-hot elements and she is burned. Look here . . .'

He turns to the young girl who is wearing on her arm a silver bangle maybe three or four inches wide like the ornaments they wear in the east. The silver grey of the bangle makes her young brown skin look as though it is glowing with health.

'Will you take off the bangle and show the man your arm?'

At first she hesitates and there is a slight frown that comes and then vanishes. Slowly she takes off the silver bangle which has been shielding her arm from view. There is a murmur of sympathy from the crowd as they see that her arm has a terrible burn where the flesh is gone almost down to the bone.

'When did this happen?' says the Boss.

'Nearly a year ago. We took her to the hospital and the arm heals for a time and then it stops. The doctors say there is something in her head that makes her as though she does not want to get better. They say because many of her friends are dead, she also wants to be dead. And I cannot bear this another day,' says the father, who has tears running down his face.

'And the demons?' says the Boss gently to the father. 'What are they?'

'They come when the tanks come; when the planes drop the bombs on houses near where we live. When her school-friend gets shot in the head in the street by the army patrol. Then the army captain comes back down the street and fires five bullets into the body of her best friend to make sure she is dead in case she is a terrorist. And her blue and white school uniform is ripped up by the bullets and covered in blood. That is when the demons come, like they come to all of us who are in this hell.'

Suddenly the father stops shouting and there is silence.

The Boss stands with his arm round the shoulder of the young girl for what seems like a long time.

'Put the silver bangle back on,' he tells her. 'On your other arm. The demons are gone.'

'And have the tanks and planes gone?' she asks him.

'No, they have not gone,' he says, 'but the demons are gone and your arm will be OK, and maybe you will not fall down any more.'

Just at that moment a woman comes up to him with a small creased photograph in her hand.

'This is my son,' she says, showing him the picture. 'In his head he had the demons and he threw himself into the fire and he was killed. Many other people were also killed. Did he do a wrong thing? Will he be punished?'

'What are the demons?' says the Boss quietly to the mother.

'What are they? They are the demons that many of the young people have. Hatred and revenge. Humiliation and despair. Anger at imprisonments with no trial and the torture. The bombs and the tanks that come in the night.

'They do not just come into our streets; they come into our heads. They take away our hope and our will to live. They possess our minds so that we are in despair. They are the demons.'

'How did your son die?' says the Boss.

'He got explosives and strapped them round him and he went to find the enemy. And he found them and they died together. Do you condemn him?'

'It is not for me to judge,' says the Boss.

'He was not an evil boy,' says the mother, 'And he did not want to die. He wanted to live and to be free. He was young and beautiful like this young woman here. But like her he was born in slavery. He never knew freedom. Every day his life was an experience of death and degradation from the invaders. For twenty-five years we waited for the world to come and help us, but no one came. The world leaders made speeches, but no one came. My son would say to me: "Mother, we are dead already. What do we have to lose!"

'Then, one day, he hears a story that changes him. The story is from the old books about a man who is very strong. One day the strong man is captured by a powerful enemy. For many years he suffers until, one day, he prays to God for greater strength. His prayer is answered, for he breaks his chains and escapes. But instead of running away, he goes right into the city of the enemy and pulls down the columns of the place where the enemy are eating and drinking. And the building comes crashing down and all his enemies are killed; and the strong man also dies.

'My son says the strong man was the first suicide bomber, even though it was many centuries ago. In a war, he said, many give their lives to defeat their enemy.

'And so my son went and did that. And I let him go.

'He was not strong. He was young and beautiful and he was training to be a doctor,' she says.

The Boss is quiet for a few moments as he thinks about the story the mother has told him. Finally he says to her: 'Mother, it is a hard thing to say to you, but bombs and violence are not the answer. We have to love our enemy. There is no other way to end this. It is the only way.'

When the Boss says this the crowd are quiet and young John says kindly to the mother: 'Whether your son was right or wrong I do not know, but maybe he laid down his life for his friends. He gave his life for his people.'

'Yes,' says the mother wearily, 'he gave his life for his people.'

Then she looks at the Boss: 'Is your mother here?'

'Yes,' says the Boss. 'She is standing next to you.'

The woman looks at the Boss's mother and says: 'You are his mother? What would you do if your beautiful son here wanted to give his life for his people? Would you let him go?'

The other woman is pale and silent for a moment, and there are tears in her eyes also. 'I would let him go,' she says at last. 'A long time ago, I let him go.'

'And not only you,' murmurs young John under his breath, as though thinking about something he heard, or maybe something he wrote in that creased little notebook he carries around. 'The Father also lets him go.'

'What are you writing?' asks the Mags, who is watching young John. He has suddenly turned away and is scribbling something down, as though he is afraid of forgetting it and it will be lost for ever.

'Just a thought,' says John.

'Can you tell me the thought?'

'God so loved the world that he gave his son. He let him go . . .'

'And?' says the Mags.

'And what?'

'Why did he let him go?'

'So that we might have life?' asks young John.

'Good boy,' says the Mags, hugging him.

The sparkle tree

The street-sweeper stands leaning on his broom and looks. And the Boss and the others all stop in silence and look. Even I, who have seen most things, stop and stare at the tree which has burst into flames.

How long they stand there I do not know, but suddenly the fire goes out and the spell is broken and the small tree stands unharmed where it had always stood. And the street-sweeper laughs out loud when he sees the faces of the gang.

'You have never seen a tree on fire before?' says the man, who has a big black moustache and whose faded tee-shirt is stained with sweat from sweeping the streets in the hot sun. 'Come with me and let me show you something.'

So the Boss and the gang walk down the street with the road-sweeper whose name is Stefan until they get to the burning tree. As they get closer something else is happening to the tree. It is not on fire now, but all over its branches there is sparkling light.

At the side of the tree is a lady who has a table covered with items that she is selling and when they get close up, the gang see what it is that makes the tree look like it is on fire and makes its branches sparkle with a dazzling light in the sun.

All along the branches the lady has hung small glass decorations in the shapes of stars and angels and other such things. The stars and angels are made out of small pieces of coloured glass joined together like crazy paving or maybe stained glass out of old buildings. As the glass ornaments move in the afternoon breeze they catch the sun, and suddenly the whole tree looks like it is ablaze.

'So,' says Stefan, 'is this not the most amazing thing?'

'Well,' says the Boss, 'this is certainly a smart way to sell these glass hanging things, which we have often seen in people's windows. And for a time it looked as though the tree was on fire and this is certainly an attention-grabbing idea, to hang these glass things on the branches of this tree in the sun. But, without wishing to give any offence, I would not say it was amazing.'

'The man is right,' says Stefan the street-sweeper with a laugh. 'A tree on fire is not so amazing, maybe: though I am not sure how many times you have seen such a thing. But what is truly amazing is this lady here who makes these glass stars and angels and I do not know what else, and hangs them on the tree to sell them to people to hang in the windows of their homes.

'For a start, do you know where this coloured glass comes from? No? Then I will tell you. It comes from the streets. When the tanks come and blow up a house or maybe a shop there is always broken glass blown into the street. I know this because I have to sweep up the mess the Army makes.

'But this lady goes out and picks up this worthless smashed-up glass and takes it home and makes it into these beautiful decoration things you see here.'

'Well,' says the Boss, 'I can see that is very clever – and I am beginning to see why it is an amazing thing that you are telling us.'

'That is good,' says Stefan, 'but for the others here who are still confused, I will spell it out. The lady makes these beautiful glass things out of the wreckage the Army leaves in the street, not just to make money to live, but as an act of courage and defiance. It is like she is saying to the Army: "You destroy our homes and break our lives in pieces, but we will not be destroyed. We will make beauty out of the ruin you bring. We will not die."

'And then she hangs these glass things in the tree so that when the tanks come past again they see the sparkling light, or maybe even the tree on fire if the sun is right, and they say: "How can this happen when we have blown up these people's homes and smashed their lives? Can we tear down every tree and grind the broken glass to dust?"

'After that the Army send people to threaten this lady and warn her not to do the things with the glass any more. And they are very angry with her. But they are also afraid because they know she will not stop – and they know they cannot win. Because all the people want is to live in peace,' says Stefan.

'That is an amazing thing,' says the Boss with great respect. 'And if you and this lady will come and eat with us I will tell you another thing which is amazing. But, before we go, I have to tell you that this tree is not looking so good and I think it may be dead and there will be no more fruit on it.'

So later on, when it is evening, the Boss and the gang and Stefan and the lady with the sparkling tree, and many poor people from round about who have heard there is food, are all gathered round the tables at an open-air café. And when they have finished eating and have had maybe several glasses of this and that, the Boss says: 'Now I will tell you the story I promised.'

Once, he says, there was a great king who decided to give a banquet. The invitations were sent out; the food was prepared and the tables were laid ready for the meal. But, one by one, the guests who had been invited all began to make excuses why they could not come to the banquet. When the king was told that not one of his invited guests had come to the big dinner he had prepared, he was very angry.

So what did the great king do? He sent his servants out into the streets and told them to invite all of the poor and the outcast, the broken and the despairing. 'They will be my guests,' he said. And so they all sat down to eat at the banquet the king had prepared.

When the Boss has finished his story it is quiet for a few moments. Then the Rox says uneasily: 'Jez, I do not wish to be disrespectful in any way but, while that is a very nice story, I would not say it was amazing.'

'Well,' says Stefan the street-sweeper, 'it is amazing if you understand it. For this great king is doing just what this lady with the sparkle tree does with the bits of smashed-up glass she finds in the street. He is going out and finding what is broken and worthless and making of it something that has beauty and value. Like the glass things hanging in the tree, it is a sign of hope and it is an amazing thing that a great king should act in this way.'

'It is a sign of hope for us, too,' calls out a voice from the back.

Everybody looks round, and one of the men who is sleeping rough on the streets stands up and points to the Boss:

'That is what this guy is doing. He finds the broken and thrown-away people and welcomes us. He gives us value like this lady does with the broken and thrown-away glass. Today is the first time that anybody ever invites me in for a meal. Most people do not even throw a coin as they pass by.

'This meal may not look much like a banquet and, with respect, you do not look much like a king. But one thing I learn in this life is that things are not always as they seem.'

A visit from the undertaker

Undertakers normally wait till you are dead. At least, those with any consideration for the feelings of the deceased. But the one that shows up to see the Boss arrives early – and, to everyone's embarrassment, in the middle of a dinner party.

Not that this dinner party is going so well, it has to be said. For a start, the invitation comes from the least likely source: one of the Robed Ones. So why should the Robed Ones want to give a dinner party for the Boss? And how will it look when word gets around he has been fraternizing with the enemy?

But the Boss says we must have generosity of spirit. So, if someone asks you to walk with them for one mile, hey, why not walk with them for two miles? And if somebody asks you to give them five pounds, then give them ten – or maybe even a twenty. And if your enemy asks you round for a meal, then maybe he is not such a bad enemy and, anyway, we are to love our enemy. And if that means showing up and eating their food and having a few beers with them, why is that such a hardship?

Now the gang, who are always sympathetic to the offer of food and a few beers, do not have a big problem with this argument. So it is agreed that the next day they will go to the big house where the guy with the black robes lives, and they will see what is on the menu: both the food and the real reason they are being invited. For it is often said that there is no such thing as a free dinner.

The next day starts off well enough but, as it gets nearer the time for the meal, things start to go wrong. The first thing that happens is that the bus back into town breaks down. The driver says it is OK and that he can fix it. But after an hour sitting in the bus in the hot afternoon sun, the gang are less certain that this thing can be fixed and maybe they will be there for ever – and miss dinner as well.

Finally it is decided they will get out and walk, even though it is a good five miles back into the town. And with the dust being kicked up by passing traffic that is not a pleasant thing. So it is that, when they finally arrive for dinner at the big house, they are tired and sweating and covered with dust.

The Mags says she needs a shower before she is having dinner with the sort of posh crowd they are going to be meeting. But this should not be a problem, for a house this big must have half a dozen bathrooms and no doubt they can have ten minutes to freshen up.

This is not how it works out, however, since the minute they ring the doorbell it is clear the host is concerned that dinner is not spoiled and they must come straight away to the table and sit down. And the Mags is muttering that this guy does not have the generosity of spirit the Boss was talking about.

Otherwise he will be saying: 'Ten minutes to freshen up? Relax. Take twenty minutes and I will tell the cook to hold the grub till you are ready. And here, take this nice clean towel and a glass of something cold and sparkling to drink, for you have had a terrible journey.'

Instead, they all sit down tired and dirty and before they can draw breath the food is on its way, served by some aged person in a dinner jacket who does not seem to like the way they look. Or maybe it is the way they smell, for the table has been set outside on the veranda, as though they would bring something unpleasant into the house if they were to use the big dining room with the crystal chandelier and the thick pile carpets.

But if the gang think the evening has got off to a difficult start, there is worse to come. As they are getting into the first course and struggling to make polite conversation, they suddenly realize another guest has shown up. But this guest is uninvited; and even less welcome than they are, by the look on the face of the host.

The uninvited guest is a young woman wearing a very short skirt and a blouse that only just seems to meet in the middle. There is a lot of her golden brown skin showing and, if the evening was not so warm, she would very likely catch a cold dressed like that. But there must be something pretty special about this lady because the gang have stopped eating, which is a very unusual thing to happen – especially when they are hungry.

The only person who has not stopped eating is the Boss: maybe because the young woman is standing behind him and he has not seen her. But the host, who is a very fat guy, has certainly seen her and knows what game she is up to. Heaving himself to his feet he yells to the servant in the dinner jacket: 'Throw this tart out onto the street right now and what the hell does she think she is up to, walking in and disgracing a person's dinner party anyway?'

The woman with the short skirt steps forward into the light and reaches out to put her hand on the Boss's shoulder. The dinner guests can see now that there are tears running down her face. Without turning round, the Boss reaches back and puts his hand on hers and pulls her gently towards him till she is standing right up against his chair and her tears are falling onto his sweat-stained shirt.

Then something very strange happens. Taking a small bottle out of her white shoulder bag, she pours something onto the Boss's head and starts to rub it slowly into his hair, massaging it gently into his scalp and down the back of his neck. Then, taking one of the expensive linen napkins from the table, she wipes his face like a mother cleaning the face of a small child. Finally she pours the last drops of the oil onto his shirt and the fragrance drifts across the veranda and out into the night.

The host is deeply offended at all these goings-on in his home and shouts at the Boss that if he knew what sort of sinful woman this is, he would not be letting her touch him in this way.

But the Boss tells the host that what the woman is doing is just fine. 'When we arrived at your house,' he says, 'you did not have the courtesy to let us freshen up; even though you knew we were dirty after a hard journey and you have a big house with many bathrooms.

'But since she came in, this woman has been washing me with her tears. And this oil that she has poured on me? She has anointed

me for my burial for she knows I am going to die. She is the undertaker – though she is a bit early,' he adds with a smile.

'She is no undertaker,' yells the host, 'she is a whore, a tart and
a prostitute. She has no place in this house, and no place being near a
man of God for she has chosen a life of sin.'

'Chosen it?' says the young woman suddenly. 'Was it my choice?'

'What else could it have been?' says the host, his face red with
anger.

'What else could I have done?' counters the woman. 'When the
soldiers break down the door and take away my husband and I never
see him again. And with him gone I have no way to feed my children.
Am I to let them starve?'

'So what happened?' says the Boss quietly, still holding her hand as
she stands beside his chair.

'So what happened is that, one day, a man comes and says he can
help. He gives me money and he is very kind. But then he says he
wants to sleep with me. I do not want to sleep with him but he says
that if I don't, there will be no more money.

'Then, later, he says I must also sleep with other men if I want the
money for my children. And since I have slept with him and my children need food and clothes, what else can I do? What do I have to lose?

'So this is the choice I make to feed my children after their father
is taken away. I know I am sinful and I am ashamed and that is why
I have come here.'

But the Boss says she has no sin; otherwise why would she be
crying when she came in?

The host does not like this at all and says that she has been sleeping with evil men. And the woman says that he is right; they are very
evil. And some of them are officers from the army of occupation and
some of them are among the religious leaders of the Robed Ones.

At this point it is becoming pretty clear that the party is over and
we should all go, for the host is shouting for someone to call the
police.

When we get outside, the Boss asks the lady: 'What is your name
and what are you going to be doing from now on?'

The woman says her name is Samantha, but her friends call her Sam. But what she is going to do in the future, she does not know. Although she might try being an undertaker after all, since there are always lots of people dying in these parts. Anyway, she says, I know quite a lot about bodies.

And the Boss says: 'Well, Sam, maybe I will be one of your first clients if you do go into the undertaking business.'

She looks at him in surprise. But he is not smiling.

Forest fire

From now on everything seems different. As though the clocks have somehow speeded up and you cannot quite catch up with what is happening. Nothing has changed on the outside: it's just that suddenly things seem to be happening a little bit faster.

A long time ago some guy says a tiny spark can kindle a great flame. And that is what seems to be happening right now. Just what the small spark is that sets this whole thing alight, I do not know. Like a forest fire: who can tell what starts the inferno?

Maybe a dropped cigarette or a bit of broken glass that catches the sun on a hot day. A moment when nothing seems to be happening. Then a tiny lick of flame and perhaps a wisp of smoke so small that nobody notices. And what fans it into life? The slightest breeze. Maybe nothing more than the air stirred for a moment by the wings of a fly.

The first thing anyone can remember is that Maria, the lady who grows the onions, is very angry. Not that this is surprising. Old Andreas, her husband of fifty-two years, has a new love in his life. Not only that, there is talk of him leaving home.

The trouble starts a few months back when he is sitting having a beer with his nephew after the market has closed for the day and they have sold all their onions. For several weeks now Andreas has been thinking the pains in his back that have kept him doubled over for years are not so bad as they were. And the swelling in the joints of his hands is also not so painful. And, all in all, Andreas is not feeling as old as he used to. Which is a very remarkable thing.

So when his nephew gets to talking about selling the rusty Datsun pick-up truck and buying a new one, Andreas has an idea. Why don't they save their money and fix up the old truck themselves? And he thinks back to when he was young like his nephew and spent his time tinkering with old cars and getting covered with engine oil and dust.

So every weekend Andreas leaves Maria and the onion patch and catches the bus. He walks through the military checkpoint and goes to the house of his nephew and there they spend many happy hours working on the old pick-up.

But this makes Maria very angry and she says that the old man should act his age and stop behaving like the young men who drive fast cars and wear sunglasses with lenses like mirrors so you cannot see where they are looking.

She says it would be bad enough if the new love of his life was a young woman with nice legs, because then she could go and give her a good slapping and tell her to leave her husband alone. But what can she do when her rival for his affections is a twenty-five-year-old busted-up truck? And why does he not leave home and go and live with his nephew so that they can work on the truck all the time, except when they are drinking cold beers in the bar in the village?

How it turns out that Andreas is feeling so young again is a mystery to Maria, but she seems to think it begins about the time some guy helps him carry his sack of onions after he was stopped at the military checkpoint. She has heard that the man who helped him is often in trouble with the authorities and she is worried Andreas is mixing with the wrong sort of people. That is why she is angry: because she is afraid. Even so, it makes her happy to see her husband can walk without being bent over and she is pleased that suddenly he seems to have a new spark of life.

Then, one weekend, Andreas tells Maria she must come with him to the house of his nephew. It is a great day. The work on the pick-up truck is finished and he wants her to see the transformation they have brought about. So Maria leaves the onion patch and goes with her husband, and sure enough, the old truck is an amazing sight.

All the dents in the body panels have been beaten out; the old bus has four brand new tyres; and the bodywork has been re-sprayed so it sparkles in the sun. Then Andreas shows Maria the engine which has been rebuilt and steam-cleaned until he says you can eat your break-fast off it. And, all in all, this looks like a pick-up truck straight out of the showroom that nobody has ever used before.

For some reason there are a lot of people in the village today and many of them are admiring the paint job on the pick-up, and Maria seems less worried that Andreas is going to get himself into trouble. In fact she has to admit the two men have done a good job on the old truck and she thinks that, if she is going to have a rival for his love, then maybe it is better it is a Datsun after all.

But, just as Maria is thinking things are going well with Andreas and there is nothing to worry about, the clocks suddenly start going a little bit faster. At first it is nothing at all. Two strangers show up and ask to speak to the owner of the pick-up.

'A friend of ours has need of your truck for a few hours,' they say to Andreas and his nephew.

'Who is it wants to use our truck?' asks the nephew. 'We have only just finished work on it and there is no way we would let anyone borrow her. And certainly not a stranger.'

'The person who needs it is the Onion Carrier,' say the two men.

'The Onion Carrier?'

'That is what we were told to say,' says one of the strangers. 'The Boss said you would understand.'

'I tell you,' says the nephew, 'this is the only person in the world I would allow to use our pick-up truck. But, for him, I would do any-thing – even though I only ever met him the once. One day he shows up and helps my uncle here carry a sack of onions, which was a very kind thing to do. But after that the old man seems to get a new lease of life. In fact, now I think about it, that is how we come to do all this work on the truck. So, not only can he borrow the truck, but I will drive it myself.'

'And I will come along, too,' says Andreas, 'just to make sure my nephew drives carefully and does not scratch the paintwork.'

By now the crowd is getting bigger and there is a lot of excitement and cheering going on, as though a celebration is taking place. The gang are there and the Boss is talking to Andreas and his nephew and saying he needs to get into the city, but with all the people, it is going to be hard to get through.

And now things are beginning to get slightly out of hand. More people are heading out of the city to meet them, because of the things they have heard about the Boss. So it is decided he will stand in the back of the pick-up so he can be seen by all the people as he enters the city.

And that is all it was. That is all that happened. Old Andreas and his nephew driving the newly painted pick-up slowly through the crowds towards the city; and people yelling and cheering and laying their coats in the road and some of them throwing flowers.

Then when they get to the military checkpoint, instead of being stopped and searched and made to wait for hours in the hot sun, the soldiers smile and wave them through. And you get the feeling this is all too easy.

The gang are following along behind the shiny red pick-up and the Rox comments on how the Boss looks like a statesman making a triumphal entry into the city, with the crowds cheering their leader. But young John has the feeling it looks like a man going to the gallows in the back of a cart called a tumbrel or something. Except the Boss doesn't have his hands tied behind his back.

As we get into the centre of the city, Andreas' young nephew leans out of the cab of the pick-up and shouts: 'Where now, Onion Carrier?'

And the Boss shouts back: 'The Citadel.'

Suddenly things are moving much too fast, and you know there is going to be trouble. And it will only take a small spark for the whole thing to go up in flames.

The alchemists

For centuries people struggled to make their fortune by turning lead into gold. While no one succeeded in this quest, some managed to go one better. They discovered how to make gold out of nothing. And one of these people is Mr Azo Varis.

Mr Varis runs a financial services company which is based, surprisingly enough, in the religious Citadel of this fine city. And every day pilgrims come from far and wide to give Mr Varis their hard-earned money.

Why this strange thing should happen, day in and day out, until Mr Varis is one of the richest people in the land, is easy to explain. Though you may feel it is hard to credit.

In order to maintain its important and prestigious role in the life of the nation, the Citadel, like any big corporation, needs money. And to get this money it charges a tax on the pilgrims, who have a religious obligation to come and pray at the Citadel. This tax is a great burden on the poorer people: yet for some strange reason it seems they are the ones who complain about it the least.

But what everybody does complain about is the way the system operates. For the Robed Ones have come up with a brilliant way of making the people pay the tax, not once – but twice. The Robed Ones insist that the tax can only be paid in the specially minted coinage of the Citadel. And who controls this special coinage? The Citadel: plus a small group of approved financial service companies. The money-changers.

So how does this make money for Mr Varis and his friends? Simply by charging commission for the money-changing service. And a very large commission fee at that. So big a commission fee that, when the pilgrims realize how much Mr Varis is taking to change their ordinary money into the special Citadel coinage, there is often a big argument and shouting and people saying things like this place is a den of thieves and not the house of prayer it is supposed to be. But, at the end of the day, they have travelled a long way and they have to pay the tax; and so they might as well pay up and shut up.

And this is how it goes, day in and day out. With Mr Varis making gold out of nothing and hiring a security van to come and take away his good fortune at the close of business.

That is how it goes: until today. Because this afternoon a red pick-up truck has stopped outside the main entrance of the Citadel where a crowd of people are suddenly gathering. The security guard outside the main portico is talking urgently on his radio as the Boss strides through the big doors of the precincts, followed by the Mags, young John and the Iscari, who is looking very worried.

Ignoring the security guards, the Boss walks straight into the courtyard where Mr Varis and other entrepreneurs are going about their lawful daily business. The courtyard is the area used by foreigners, who are not allowed to go further into the more holy parts of the Citadel. So the only place these people can say their prayers is in this courtyard where the money men are making gold out of nothing.

But it seems they find it hard to say their prayers with all the pushing and shoving and arguing that is going on over the money-changing and the other things that are happening there.

And this is what seems to be getting the Boss fired up. For not only are these foreign people forbidden access to the more holy parts of the Citadel, when the love of God is freely given to all; but the place the Robed Ones allow them to gather is like a cattle market where no one can be at peace and give thanks to God, unless of course they are stone deaf and have their eyes tight shut.

But the Boss is not deaf and his eyes are wide open and it looks like he is about to get arrested. For, no sooner does he get into the court-yard of the money-makers than he starts to kick the hell out of them and turn over their tables and throw their precious money around the place. Also he is telling them a few things about what this place is for and how they have made it a robbers' cave, just like the pilgrims have been saying.

And Mr Varis and his colleagues are demanding to know who gives him the right to treat them in this way; and they are pointing out how they provide a legitimate financial service to the pilgrims.

Meanwhile, someone has called the security guards who are trying to push their way through the crowds. But the people are not so keen to let them through, because they are pleased that at last someone has the courage to speak out about this corruption and greed.

Eventually, with the help of the crowd, the Boss gets back out into the street where the rest of the gang have been waiting. The guys are saying we should get out of town and lie low until the fuss has died down, but we have to wait for the Iscari, who seems to have disappeared. Someone says he is talking to one of the Citadel staff and trying to smooth things over. But, in any case, the Boss is not interested in leaving town.

While the rest of the gang are discussing what should happen next, he suddenly walks across the street and starts talking to a young guy who appears to be blind.

Looking back on what happened, I am surprised it is actually not the riot in the Citadel which is the spark that lights the blue touchpaper. The thing that starts the forest fire is some stupid throw-away remark the blind guy makes. Almost as a joke.

But, like a throw-away cigarette end, that throw-away remark is the small thing that sparks off the inferno.

Personally, I do not understand why at such a difficult moment the Boss has to stop and talk to anybody in the street. There have been blind people and lame people and sick people in their hundreds in the past. But, while the secret police are maybe planning to send a couple of jeeps to arrest him, the Boss has to stop and talk. And not only talk.

Before we know what is happening, he does a very strange thing. He picks up some earth and spits into his hand a few times. Then he mixes the earth into a paste.

'Close your eyes,' he tells the blind guy.

'Why close my eyes? I cannot see anyhow,' says the man.

But he closes his eyes and the Boss gently smears the mud onto his eyelids. I am amazed he can do this so gently and calmly when only minutes ago he has been hurling chairs and tables around in the Citadel.

'How does that feel?' says the Boss.

'Gritty. Strange. I feel stupid with mud on my face. Are you making a fool of me?'

'What else do you feel?'

The young guy laughs.

'I feel free. All my life people try to get me to see and I cannot do it. Now you cover my eyes with mud so I cannot see even if I wanted to. For once I cannot fail.'

'And?'

'Maybe I feel at peace in my darkness. But I cannot go around for ever with mud on my eyes.'

'You are right. You need to go and wash it off.'

'When?'

'Whenever you want. Do you want to wash it off?'

The young guy thinks some more.

'Not yet. While it is on I am safe. But when I wash it off I will still be blind.'

'Maybe,' says the Boss.

Then the Boss says goodbye and walks away with the gang, who are now very anxious that we get moving to a place of safety.

Later, we hear rumours that there has been more trouble at the Citadel and that the Boss is to blame. The blind guy has been arrested and brought before the Council of the Robed Ones. It turns out that he goes and washes his face; not in some quiet place, but right in the city centre where the fountains used to be, but where there is now just an ornamental pool. And when he washes his face, he discovers he can see.

But that is not the problem. What causes the trouble is that the crowds are so pumped up, what with the Boss coming into the city like a head of state and then the riot in the Citadel, that they are starting to get out of control.

Realizing the situation is escalating, the Robed Ones have the blind guy pulled in for questioning. And that is when it all goes wrong. They keep on asking the young man how it comes about that he can see, and they even drag in his parents to find out whether their son was blind at all.

Then, in the middle of all this, the young guy loses his temper.

'Why do you keep asking me all these questions?' he says. 'Do you also want to become a disciple of the guy who healed me?'

There is dead silence in the council room. Not because the young man has been disrespectful, but because one or two of the Robed Ones have been thinking they would actually quite like to be disciples of the Boss.

The silence is broken only by the lazy buzzing of a fly. Among the Council a sudden realization dawns: they are divided among themselves.

The leader of the Robed Ones abruptly dismisses the hearing. The young man and his parents are thrown out. Then several of the most senior Robed Ones go into a back room to talk.

'We must stay united or we are lost,' says the leader. 'We have to act fast before it is too late. The trouble-maker has to be dealt with.'

The fire has started.

The man who blinked

Maybe in a different life he would have been a poker player. Certainly the Boss has a lot of nerve when it comes to taking risks. But the strange thing is that, while he thinks gambling is a mug's game, it is as though he is engaged in the biggest gamble of all. Gambling with his life.

Every day that goes by, his battle with the Robed Ones seems to become more dangerous. At first they thought they could scare him off with a warning. But the Boss just kept on raising the stakes.

Time and time again they would show up to see what he was doing. It was clear they were trying to intimidate him. As though they were trying to stare him out. But the Boss never blinked. In fact he adopted that annoying strategy poker players use of just smiling across the table.

It was as though he knew what cards the other people held; and they weren't good enough. He knew how the game was going to end: so there was no need to worry.

Today someone else can also see how the game might end: but, unlike the Boss, he is extremely worried. The Iscari is not normally one to take risks. He likes to know where things are and where they are going to stay. For a long time now he has been very unhappy.

'The Boss is going too far,' he told the Rox one day. 'This is going to end in disaster. He has no sense of strategy. There are ways of doing things: compromise and diplomacy get you further than confrontation. We need to back off. At least for a time.'

Although the Rox is loyal to the Boss, he can see the point. He too is worried about the way things are going. Not many days back he tried to talk the Boss out of coming south into the city. But his concern for the Boss's safety ended with them having a bitter row.

But the Rox was only trying to look out for the Boss and warn him of danger. Perhaps he said the wrong thing: or perhaps it was the wrong time. But he is not disloyal.

It could be that, in the same sort of way, the Iscari is also trying to protect the Boss and safeguard the whole venture. He is not a trouble-maker: quite the opposite. He wants things to be safe. To build security as well as success into the project. But, instead, things seem to be careering out of control.

For a long time he agonizes over what to do. Then a plan gradually takes shape in his mind. It is not without danger, but it could be the only way to avert disaster.

Later that night he finds himself sitting at a table in a dimly lit room. It is the second time that day he has been inside the Citadel and he is scared. Across the table sits one of the Robed Ones. Somewhere, hidden in the shadows, the Iscari senses someone else in the room.

Like a gambler at the poker table, he makes his opening bid.

'You need to silence the Boss,' he says. 'But if you kill him there will be an uprising. He will become a martyr. You do not want that. He needs bringing to his senses. Made to back off. If you arrest him and threaten him maybe he will change course.'

'Perhaps you are right,' says a quiet voice from across the table.

'You know I am right,' says the Iscari, feeling a bit more confident.

Somewhere in the room there is a fly.

'And what is in it for you?' asks the voice.

'He needs a shock to make him realize this cannot go on. He needs saving from himself,' says the Iscari. 'It has gone too far.'

'So you want us to help you? A strange request.'

'But in your own interests,' says the Iscari.

Suddenly there is another voice from the shadows. 'No. Not in our interests. It is better to leave him. If he is who they say he is, then nothing can stop him. If he is not, then this nonsense will come to an end anyway.'

The Iscari is dimly aware that the voice from the shadows is famil-iar. Sunlight. A man at the lakeside shouting. A man whose daughter is dying.

'Meanwhile he is destroying us,' cuts in the voice at the table angrily. 'He is challenging everything. He is creating a new world. He has nothing and yet he has authority. He is dangerous – maybe he is insane. But the people do not think so. He will bring ruin upon us. He will be the death of us.'

'He gave me life,' says the voice from the shadows quietly.

'He needs stopping,' insists the voice at the table.

'He needs bringing to his senses,' says the Iscari, less scared now.

'And how do you suggest we arrest this man when he is always surrounded by the crowds?' asks the voice at the table, calm once more after the outburst. 'There would be a riot. We need to get him when he is alone.'

There is silence as the Iscari ponders the unasked question. He looks across the table into the eyes of the Robed One.

And then he blinks.

'At night he goes out to a quiet place to pray. Away from the crowds. I know where he goes. I have been there. I am his friend. I will lead you there. It will be easy.'

No one speaks.

'I can take you to him.'

For a long time there is silence.

A thick brown envelope is pushed quietly across the table towards the Iscari.

'No,' he says. 'This is not about money. He needs to be made to see sense.'

'Of course,' says the quiet voice. 'It is not about money. But I am sure you can use a little help anyway.'

'We are making a big mistake,' says the voice from the shadows.

'We are doing what is necessary. If this carries on it will bring the wrath of the military down on us all. We need to protect ourselves. Don't you understand? It is expedient that one person is removed for the good of the whole people.'

'If you kill him it will be the end of everything,' says the voice from the shadows.

'Who is speaking of death? As this friend of his says, we do not want a martyr. We are simply talking about his removal.'

'Removal where?' says the Iscari.

'To a safe place. Somewhere a long way away.'

The Iscari is looking at the envelope. Maybe he is thinking how the money could help the cause.

The fly has settled on the table.

The Iscari hesitates for a moment. Then he picks up the envelope and goes out into the night.

The dinner party

If it had not been so tragic, it would have been funny. Although we did not know it, we were into the last hours. The whole thing was coming apart and death was in the air.

And in the middle of all that, there was an argument over something and nothing: who should sit where at a dinner party.

It had been a strange day, as though a storm was coming. The Boss said we should all have a meal together that evening, although we were not sure who would be there. After the trouble at the Citadel, many people had disappeared. Lying low: sensing there may be worse to come. And, who knows, maybe they were wise to stay out of sight.

In the end it was Sophie, the wise woman as the Boss calls her, who went off to find a restaurant and make the arrangements.

When we got there we found tables had been set in an upstairs room. Four tables arranged in a square; five chairs along each side, as I remember. Flowers had been set out on the table opposite the door, maybe indicating this was the top table. The guys certainly thought so.

As the rest of the gang entered the room an argument started over who should sit at the top table. Predictably it ended up with the Rox and four of the others in the places of honour.

But then they realized they hadn't left a place for the Boss, so there was another argument about who should give up his seat. By this time the rest of the boys were all sitting down and nobody wanted to move. Fortunately the Boss and young John were still downstairs in the bar talking to the manager, so they missed most of the argument.

When the Boss finally did appear, he saw the boys had taken the seats across the top table and three-quarters of the way down each side of the square. He smiled as he noticed they had left the seats down by the door for the women.

'Hey,' the Rox calls out to the Boss. 'Sit up here with us.'

Though, by the look of it, he himself is not planning to give up his seat, and for a moment there seems to be some confusion as to where Jez is going to sit.

But the Boss says it is OK and he will sit here at the table by the door with the women and young John.

The Rox is about to start arguing with this when there is a knock on the door and, to everyone's surprise, who should walk in but Sam the undertaker with her two young children.

'I am sorry I am late,' says Sam, who is wearing a nice long dress. 'I've brought the little ones. Can we join you?'

The Boss jumps up and gives her a big hug and says this is just the time for the undertaker to show up, and he says hello to the two little girls who are called Molly and Hannah. And after they have a little chat about this and that, as girls do, they all sit down together at the table near the door with young John and Mary the Mags and Sophie.

Suddenly this whole thing seems to be getting out of shape because the table where the guys are sitting is looking less important, despite the nice flower arrangements. And the table where the Boss and Hannah and Molly and the other girls are sitting seems to be where the action is. Even though there is an empty chair, which makes the whole thing look somewhat incomplete.

But now the attention of the gang is focused on the waitress who has appeared through the door carrying a large carafe of wine which she puts down on the table in front of the Boss. At this, the Boss becomes thoughtful and, after a few moments, he stands up.

'I am glad the undertaker has arrived,' he says, 'because we may be needing someone in her line of business before too long. What I have to tell you is that this is the last time I will drink wine with you. That is, until I drink it with you in the Kingdom.'

Some of the gang are still not sure what this Kingdom is, but they are heartened at the news that there will be wine when they get there. But the Boss is still talking and it is sounding serious.

Finally, he does a strange thing. He takes some bread from the table and breaks it. 'This is my body,' he tells them. He passes it round for them all to share and Sam breaks some off for the girls.

Eventually the broken bread reaches the men at the end of the table, who until now have been feeling somewhat left out. But the Boss is not finished.

Taking the wine he pours some out. 'This is my blood, shed for many,' he tells them. And the wine is passed round the table.

After that there is an uncomfortable silence. The Rox wants to ask what all this means. But in his heart he knows.

Just then the door opens and the waitress comes back in with the food; but as she walks past, the Boss notices she is not looking too good.

'You OK?' he asks quietly.

'Yes,' says the waitress. 'Just a bit tired.'

'When do you eat?'

'Oh, when I get home.'

'That late?' says the Boss.

Without another word, he gets up from the table and walks out of the room.

But a couple of minutes later he is back, and I know he is up to something.

'The manager says you can have the rest of the evening off,' he tells the waitress. 'And we would be very happy if you would join us for dinner. See, we have even saved a place for you.'

'But who is going to serve the food?' says the waitress, sitting down in some confusion between the Mags and young John.

'I will be the waiter,' says the Boss. 'I am always telling the gang I am their servant, but I am not sure they ever listen; maybe this will convince them. And do not worry: I will pass any tips on to you.'

With the Boss waiting at table the mood of the evening picks up and pretty soon everyone is having a good time and almost forgetting the trouble there has been. So no one notices the Iscari slip out of the room. Later, when they realize he is gone, someone says that maybe

163

he will be sorting out the bill because he always likes money things in good order.

But this is odd, because Sophie has already paid for the meal when she goes to see the restaurant manager earlier in the day.

So it could be the Iscari has just gone outside for a breath of fresh air.

The arrest

Drink often brings out the worst in people. But with the Rox it is different. After a few glasses of wine he loves everybody – especially the Boss. As they stand on the pavement outside the restaurant he is earnestly telling the Boss how he and the boys will always stand by him. They will even die for him.

But the Boss hasn't had so much to drink. 'Rox,' he says, 'before the night is out you will have denied you even know me. Not once but three times.'

This distresses the Rox greatly and he assures the Boss they will always stand together, whatever happens, and nothing will ever come between them.

But just then something does come between them because Sam's two little girls come running up to say it is long past their bed-time, but they want a kiss before they go home. And Sam comes over and gives the Boss a big hug and kisses him on both cheeks; though why she is crying, nobody knows.

As this is happening, Andy suddenly remembers where he has seen her before. He turns to the Rox: 'You know who she is, don't you?'

'Of course I do,' says the Rox. 'She's the woman who showed up at the party at the big house and got us all thrown out.'

'No, before that,' says Andy. 'I saw her picture in the paper. She's the woman who pulled the Robed One out of the minefield.'

Meanwhile the Boss is saying he needs to take a walk and do some thinking and he asks the gang to come along as well. But some of the guys feel it is too dangerous with the security forces on the look-out for him. And for them as well.

The Rox says they should just go back to the lodging place and stay out of sight, for what use is it for the Boss to risk his life by being seen about the city at this time of night?

But Jez is in a serious mood and nothing is going to stop him and he tells the gang that no one is going to take his life from him, whatever happens. He says he is laying down his life of his own accord.

The gang are relieved to see the Boss is still in control: but they do not like this talk of him laying down his life. As the Boss sets off, they reluctantly follow on behind.

Eventually they come to a wooded hillside overlooking the city.

'Stay here and wait for me,' says the Boss. 'And stay awake.'

Then he goes off on his own until he comes to a clearing. It is dark and, from where I am, it is hard to see what is happening. He kneels down and looks to be praying. He stays like that for a long time, but something really bad is troubling him. The sweat is running off him so that, at first, it looks like blood. The guy is in anguish as though he is struggling with his own demons, and I am sure I hear him saying something about 'let this thing pass from me'. At last the conflict seems to be over for, after what seems like an age, he says quite clearly: 'Not my will but yours be done.'

As he is on his knees praying there is a fly somewhere nearby, but in the darkness I cannot see where it is.

There is someone else there as well: a figure standing among the trees. As the Boss falls silent, a shadow moves across the clearing and I see that it is a woman with a cloak over her shoulders. She stands beside him for a moment in the darkness. She reaches out and strokes his hair as if to calm him. Then she turns and walks silently away into the night.

As she goes I am sure it is Sophie, but I cannot see too well in the dark. One thing I do remember is thinking that, for an instant, the cloak looks like the wings of a bird spread over him as she reaches out to touch his head. Or maybe I dreamed the whole thing and it was nothing but the breeze.

Whatever happened, he finally gets up and makes his way slowly back to where the gang are waiting.

Perhaps it is the big meal or the drink, but when he gets there he finds them all asleep. They wake up when they realize he is back; but by then it is too late. Before they can say anything, there is the sound of marching feet. Suddenly we are confronted by a detachment of soldiers with fixed bayonets.

'Run for it,' someone yells and the gang scatter, crashing blindly through the trees, leaving the Boss alone in the darkness. I notice the Iscari is there with the soldiers. But, as they are pushing the Boss into the back of one of the jeeps, he too runs off into the night.

I follow the jeeps back into the city. The night is still. It is getting cold.

For an hour or so nothing seems to happen.

Suddenly I spot the Rox. He is hanging around outside the court-yard of the Citadel where something is going on, even though it is the middle of the night. From where I am perched on a roof-top, I can hear people arguing. The Boss is being questioned by some of the Robed Ones. Outside in the courtyard a small crowd has gathered.

How the Rox has discovered where they are holding the Boss, I do not know; but I reckon he must be crazy to go anywhere near the Citadel on a night such as this.

It is the early hours of the morning by now and I can see the Rox has slipped into the courtyard and is standing at the back near a fire someone has lit. He warms his hands and stares across towards the room where the interrogation is taking place. Someone comes over to him and speaks but he shakes his head and looks away.

Later someone else comes up and talks to him but again he shakes his head and walks off. Finally two young women walk over, and it looks as though an argument is starting; for suddenly the Rox shouts out in a voice everyone can hear: 'I tell you, I do not know him.'

Everybody stops and turns. Even the interrogation in the big room that opens onto the courtyard stops for a moment. And I am sure I glimpse the Boss turn and look towards his friend.

Suddenly the Rox realizes what he has done. He gives a great cry of pain and runs out of the courtyard. Later I see him standing by the wall of the Citadel sobbing.

He has his hands over his ears as if to block out the sound of his own voice and is banging his head against the stonework, howling like a creature in torment.

The fury of the mob

It is a terrible thought that, while people go about their daily lives without a care in the world, hidden from sight behind the façade of a public building something horrifying is happening.

In a large stone cellar, below the grand reception rooms with their oak panelling and thick pile carpets, a man is being interrogated. Tied to a chair, his face bloody from the blows he has received. Hour after hour the questioning continues. A bag is placed over his head and tied so tightly round his neck he thinks he will suffocate in the darkness. They start beating him with pieces of wood, fists, truncheons. Urine stains the floor and the smell of sweat fills the room.

Finally the bag is ripped off. Water is thrown over the prisoner. Painfully he regains consciousness. Outside, dawn is breaking but the man's spirit is not broken. He will not confess. He will not retract what he has said and done. They have failed.

But others will not fail. The interrogators leave the room to consult. Half an hour later, the prisoner is dragged outside to a waiting car. As they drive away, people are going to work; waiting for a bus; buying a morning paper; chatting in the street. Not seeing; not hearing. A different world.

It is certainly a different world at Mr Mammon's trans-global corporation, where this morning something very unusual is happening. The staff have just been told they can all have the day off. Tomorrow is a religious festival, says Mr Mammon, and it is fitting that people should have time to prepare for the celebrations. But this is very strange, for Mr Mammon's only religion is money and the last thing he is going to do is give a day off to the people who make him that money.

But there it is: a free holiday. The only condition is that they come along to the city square later in the morning. There will be something well worth seeing, says the generous Mr Mammon.

Meanwhile, the car has reached the offices of the Regional Governor, Mr Charles J. Pontus, who is the ruler of this country on behalf of the army of occupation.

A detachment of soldiers appears and the prisoner is dragged into the military headquarters. They are followed by a group of Robed Ones, including their leader.

Outside in the city square, a crowd has started to gather. As word of the arrest spreads, more people begin to arrive. Most are ordinary city folk, but some seem to be from Mr Mammon's company.

Although they have phoned ahead and explained that this is an extremely serious matter, the Robed Ones find that, when they arrive at the military headquarters, Mr Pontus is not there to greet them. The Regional Governor likes to keep people waiting: it reminds them who is in charge.

Finally, the Robed Ones and their prisoner are admitted to a large audience chamber where the Regional Governor is sitting in a high-backed chair like an examining magistrate.

'Who is the prisoner?' he demands; and the Boss is pushed forward.

'A man claiming to be a king,' says the leader of the Robed Ones. 'A man who threatens the stability of the region. He causes unrest. He is a trouble-maker and a law-breaker.'

'What do you wish me to do with him?'

'Remove him. Get rid of him. He is an enemy of the empire.'

'His crime?'

There is a pause and whispered conversation among the Robed Ones.

'He has opposed the payment of taxes.'

Charles J. Pontus smiles. 'Taxes? Money is certainly a serious matter: to accountants. My concern is whether this man is a threat to security.'

'He claims to be a king. And his influence is spreading.'

'And you want him silenced?'

'Yes.'

'Dead?'

'Silenced.'

'We want him dead,' says one of the Robed Ones suddenly. There is a murmur of voices as some agree, but others are saying that is going too far.

Sensing that any difference of opinion among themselves may weaken their case, the leader of the Robed Ones intervenes:

'Sir, consider the implications. The possible consequences. What will the Press say about it if you let this man go?'

'Am I ruled by the media?' snaps Pontus.

'Of course not, but it may be interpreted as a sign of weakness if he goes free. It may encourage other trouble-makers. Think of the headlines. Public opinion. Your superiors. This is not just a religious issue; it is about public order. And we must maintain order and stability.'

Pontus stands up abruptly: 'I will question the man myself.'

The others are ushered out of the room.

He is alone with the prisoner for a long time.

Finally the Robed Ones are summoned back into the audience chamber.

'I find no charge for this man to answer,' says Pontus, looking round at the accusers with contempt. 'Utterly no reason for a death sentence. Take him away and set him free.'

'The people will not accept that,' shouts the leader of the Robed Ones. 'There will be a riot. An uprising. He must be removed.'

'An uprising among the people?' says Pontus. 'Well, let us consult the people.'

He walks towards the door and the Robed Ones follow him out onto the steps of the military headquarters. The prisoner is brought out and is made to stand in front of the crowd. There is a murmur of unease as the people see the blood on his face.

Pontus is handed a microphone and addresses the crowd, which by now is numbering getting on for a thousand.

'This man has been brought before me on the very serious charge of subversion,' shouts Pontus. 'However, I have examined the accusations against him most thoroughly and . . .'

He pauses so his words will have maximum effect.

'. . . I find nothing to support the charges. He has done nothing to deserve punishment, and certainly not death. I therefore propose to have him released.'

For a moment there is silence among the crowd. Then someone shouts: 'Death. He must die.'

Others take up the cry: 'Death. Death. Death.'

The leader of the Robed Ones steps across to the Regional Governor and speaks urgently:

'I am not sure death is appropriate. We do not want a martyr. He must simply be removed. Silenced.'

Pontus nods and addresses the crowd again.

'I know there are strong feelings about this man,' he shouts, 'but we must observe due process and the rule of law. A man cannot be sentenced to death other than by the law. I have questioned this man and his accusers and I find no case to answer. I will therefore release him.'

But this seems only to enrage the crowd as though something is fanning the flames, and the cry goes up again: 'Death. Death. Death.'

And this time the leader of the Robed Ones and some of the others are joining in the cry as though they are suddenly being swept along by the overwhelming roar of fury.

Pontus tries a third time to speak but it is as though he is facing a wall of fire. Suddenly he knows he is beaten. Not only that; there is every chance this will turn into a riot if something is not done. Though what has sparked such anger in the crowd, he cannot quite work out.

Instead Pontus turns to an aide, who goes away and returns with a bowl of water and a towel.

The crowd are hushed by this strange development. While there is quiet in the city square, Pontus shouts out to the people defiantly: 'I wash my hands of this man's blood.'

He turns and issues another order. Moments later a large squad of soldiers appears, lining up in front of the prisoner. But these are not the usual young conscripts who guard the military checkpoints. These are battle-hardened troops.

The crowd are suddenly silent as the prisoner is pushed into the back of a large black van and the doors slammed shut. The Mags and several of the others who have been among the crowd turn away. They do not notice a white limousine which at that moment is gliding silently out of the city square.

The Place of the Skull

Maybe the rest is better left unsaid. The things that happened still seem too terrible to speak. I realize we have started talking of him as the prisoner, as though he does not have a name. As though there is a distance between us, and he is no longer the one held in our affection. Or maybe it is because we cannot bear to speak of those things happening to one we have loved. And still love.

But he would want it told. One day he said he was the way, the truth and the life. The way, the truth and the death might have been more fitting. But anyway: the truth. Maybe the truth of God.

They do not take him far. Just out of the city to a military airfield. There is an old aircraft hangar used for sports; an indoor football pitch with rows of seats round it, creating an arena. The whole battalion is there: every seat is filled. These are hard men but, even so, there is a buzz of excitement. It is not often they see blood sport.

Outside the van pulls up and the prisoner is dragged out into the dust of the airfield. He blinks in the strong sunlight for a moment, but then the guards push him violently through the doors and into the great metal hangar.

There is a shout of applause from the soldiers as he is led to the centre of the arena. There he is shackled. His blood-stained clothing is torn off until he is naked. As each piece of clothing comes away there is a roar of excitement.

Then a heavily built soldier steps forward, and it begins. Sharp pieces of bone and metal fastened to the thongs of the whip tear into the prisoner's flesh so that after the first few strokes his back is ripped open. The crowd are screaming in a mad rage – or maybe something else.

174

I do not know how long this goes on. Maybe twenty or thirty strokes that rip into the body of the man who is our friend. Maybe it was forty strokes. And then it stops.

But now the crowd are in a frenzy. The heavily built soldier has thrown down the whip and something else is happening. A rhythmic chanting and clapping begins; slowly at first but gradually rising to a deafening crescendo. I cannot bear to look at what is happening out there.

Finally the noise subsides. Something new has started. Into the arena come three more soldiers, walking as if in solemn procession. One is carrying a purple robe. The second carries a heavy marching-stick, the sort drill sergeants use to measure the length of a soldier's stride. The third carries a circle of desert thorns.

The prisoner is unshackled and stands unsteadily before the ranks of soldiers.

'Behold your king!' shouts the heavily built one. 'I have already given him my homage.'

There is a roar of laughter at the joke.

'Now you will pay him yours.'

The purple robe is placed round the shoulders of the prisoner.

Then the circle of thorns is rammed onto his head, tearing open the skin at the temples. The blood runs slowly down and into his eyes.

Finally, the measuring-stick is thrust into his hand.

'Hail to the king,' shouts the soldier.

'Hail to the king,' roar the crowd.

'And what do we do with kings?' shouts the soldier. 'We knock 'em down.'

Saying this, he grabs the measuring-stick and, swinging it like a club, smashes it against the prisoner's head.

There is a splintering crack that can be heard across the hangar. For a moment there is silence. Then more shouting and yelling as the prisoner collapses on the floor.

Suddenly a senior officer appears.

The prisoner is dragged to his feet and the purple robe is removed. His own clothes are hastily replaced. An escort of six soldiers appears and he is led stumbling to the hangar door.

*

And now we have come to the last. Why they call it the Place of the Skull I do not know, but it is well named. A place of humiliation and death. A place of execution.

Low cloud is rolling in from the west and the sky has darkened, although it is still only mid-day.

As they fastened him to the cross-beam he cried out. Not at the nails or his torn flesh; but when his head fell back against the wood-work. The men who hammered at his hands and feet glanced up at each other in silence and hoped he would not die before their work was finished.

Two other prisoners are being executed with him.

Now the prisoner hangs, arms outstretched. The body's weight begins to slowly crush the rib-cage inwards. Breathing becomes more difficult. They have left the circle of thorns on his head, but now the blood has dried.

An hour passes: maybe two. Maybe a thousand years. Among the crowd stand the women; stricken and helpless. The Mags, Sophie and the mother. With them young John and another woman they do not know, but who young John seems to remember. Further off, a Robed One stands alone, watching. In the distance, an old man who once was blind.

As the prisoner hangs, the sinews twist and tear. It is cold.

Then the man slowly raises his head and cries out:

'My God. My God. Why have you forsaken me?'

He is silent but, like an echo, the Mags speaks quietly, as if to herself:

'. . . and are so far off . . . but I will praise you . . . for you have heard the voice of him who cries . . . and is afflicted . . .'

'What is that?' asks young John.

'A prayer. From the holy books. A cry of despair. And maybe of hope.'

'Is that what he was saying?'

'I do not know.'

A light rain has started to fall and it is getting colder.

As the women watch in silence, a small bird is circling distractedly overhead. It settles on the cross-beam near the prisoner's head. There is blood in the man's matted hair.

Maybe it is the movement of the wings, but the man once more raises his head: the words come clearly on the breeze.

'Forgive. Father, forgive them. They do not know what they do.'

The Mags puts her arm silently round young John and she can feel him sobbing.

'Why has he let this happen?' she says.

'To show there are no limits,' says John. 'Not even this.'

Suddenly there is a terrible cry from the prisoner; and the body relaxes

A fly settles on the blood-soaked corpse.

For a long time there is silence.

It is raining steadily now.

In the distance a military radio crackles into life. The officer in charge of the execution detail listens. The festival begins in three hours; the executions must be completed by then. He issues a brief order.

A soldier strides across. A bayonet is fixed to his rifle in case there is trouble from the crowd. When he comes to the prisoner he sees he is already dead; but to make sure he plunges the bayonet deep into the man's side. The rain is heavy now. It washes the blood down the body in rivulets.

The Robed One who has been watching from a distance turns abruptly away and walks to his car. It takes him some time to drive into the city. The holiday traffic is heavy and it is late when he arrives at the military headquarters.

'Name?' snaps the orderly at the reception desk.

'Jenkins. Jenkins-Russell.'

'Russell Jenkins.'

'Jenkins-Russell.'

The soldier frowns at the Robed One.

'Go in.'

Mr Pontus is surprised to see the Robed One, and even more surprised that the prisoner is already dead.

'You are sure?'

'Quite sure.'

'How?'

'It is said there was an incident while he was in custody. Some sort of head injury.'

'Why have you come?'

'To ask for the body.'

'The body? Why do you want the body? You have already taken his life.'

'It is not for me. It is for his friends.'

Mr Pontus is silent for a long time.

'It is a bad day. He should not have died.'

'I know.'

The Regional Governor writes something down on a card.

'This is a release permit. Guard the body well.'

'We will make the grave secure.'

'No,' snaps Mr Pontus, 'I will make the grave secure. Go now. I will arrange an escort.'

When Mr Jenkins-Russell gets back to the Place of the Skull, the women are taking down the body. It is still warm.

The Mags thinks back to another time when she held him.

As she steps back to lay the body down, she feels the slightest movement under her foot. As though a fragment of egg shell has been crushed.

She looks down.

'What?' says John.

'Nothing. A fly. I trod on it.'

By the time they reach the grave the rain has stopped.

'Why do you have an empty tomb?' the mother asks the woman who is with them.

'It was for a friend,' says the woman. 'But they never released the body.'

Just then there is the sound of an army truck approaching. As the body is laid in the grave, the soldiers winch two large concrete blocks from the back of the lorry.

'Our orders are to seal the grave,' says one of the men. 'Regional Governor's instructions.'

The Mags smiles to herself.

'What?' says young John.

'I was thinking: he has somewhere to lay his head now.'

As the army truck drives away the women and young John are left with Mr Jenkins-Russell at the graveside.

'What happens now?' says young John.

'Nothing happens,' says the Mags. 'It is finished.'

Another death

Maybe this is how an avalanche starts. A single pebble gets dislodged; perhaps by the rain or some small creature. Then another and another, until the whole hillside suddenly comes crashing down.

That is how it seems the next morning. For a long time there is silence. Most of them have not slept. No one speaks. The dawn has come hours ago but no one has noticed.

There is a quiet knock at the door. It is Andy with yet more terrible news. As if there could be more.

He sits at the table and looks round at the others:

'He is dead,' he says. 'The Iscari is dead.'

'How?' says young John.

'Hanged. So they say.'

'Poor boy. Poor, dear boy.'

For a moment there is silence. Then the Mags begins to cry. Quietly at first.

It is as though the sound of her sobbing breaks the spell of silence and suddenly everyone is in tears. The women and young John are crying but the Rox slams out and shuts himself in a bedroom. Through the door they can hear him howling like an animal in pain.

But no one goes to him. Their pain is too great, and maybe too much has happened.

Finally, after a long time, the fury of the storm begins to pass. In the bedroom there is the sound of slow, retching sobs. Sophie puts the kettle on and young John is sitting with the Mags.

'I can't stop thinking about him. He will be cold in that grave,' she says through her tears.

'No, he will not be cold.'

'All night alone in the dark. With none of us there. Will he be lonely?'

'No. He will not be lonely,' says young John. 'It is just us who will be lonely.'

'We will never see him again.'

'No.'

'I want to go back. At least be there. Near him.'

'Maybe. Later. We are near him now.'

'Why did he do it, John? Why did he let it happen?'

'I don't know. Maybe to show us God's love. A love stronger than death. To show us God's love will not bow to anything.'

'But it wasn't God who suffered.'

'Don't we feel the pain? And what about his mother? Isn't she suffering?'

'So, is God suffering?'

Sophie puts two mugs of tea on the table and walks quietly back to the kitchen.

'I don't know whether God is suffering,' says young John. 'But that's how it feels.'

'Why did he have to die?'

'I don't know. Perhaps it was inevitable, given the way the world is.'

'It all started a long time back,' says the Mags. 'The writing was on the wall the day he touched the leper. It started then.'

'He said he had been sent to bring good news to the poor.'

'But he didn't say what it would cost.'

'Well they've got him where they wanted him. Out of the way.'

'Same place they want the poor. Buried. Out of sight.'

They sit for a long time in silence.

'What do we do now, John?'

'I don't know. Remember him. Make sure we don't lose the vision. Don't forget him.'

She smiles and shakes her head.

Sophie comes over and joins them.

'How are the boys?' asks the Mags.

'Not very good,' says Sophie. 'They feel terrible about running away. And then staying in hiding when it came to the end. And there's something really big going on with the Rox, but he won't talk about it. Anyway, at least some of us were there with him at the end.'

'What about the Iscari?' says young John.

'I don't know. Some people are saying he hanged himself.'

'Why? What happened?' says the Mags.

Sophie is silent for a moment.

'It looks as though he told the Robed Ones where to find him.'

'But he didn't need to do that,' says young John. 'They could have found him themselves: it would just have taken them longer. Anyway, why would the Iscari want him dead? He loved him. We all loved him.'

'I'm not sure he did want him dead,' says Sophie. 'Who knows what was going on in his head? Anyway, nobody mentioned death until the crowd suddenly turned on him. After that everybody seemed to get the blood lust. They suddenly wanted a lynching.'

'Well, they got one,' says young John bitterly. 'But he saw it coming. Remember him saying he was laying down his life; and no one was taking it from him?'

Just then there is a light tapping at the window. It is Sam. Moments later she joins them.

'I heard,' she says. 'I'm so sorry. He saved my life. I still don't know how I'm going to tell the girls.'

'Tea?' says Sophie.

'Coffee, if you've got it. Black, no sugar.'

'He loved you,' says the Mags.

'He loved everybody,' says Sam. 'Even the Robed Ones and the soldiers.'

'It's good of you to come,' says John. 'But it's dangerous. You need to stay away.'

'I had to come,' says Sam. 'You're like family. How could I not come? Anyway there's something I need to talk to you about.'

Sophie puts a mug of coffee in front of Sam and sits down with them:

'What is it?'

Sam pauses for a moment. 'I want to go to the grave. I'm going to wash him and make him nice. I've got some stuff.'

'What stuff?' asks John.

'Nice-smelling stuff. I can't bear to think of him lying there in the state he must have been in last night.'

She pauses, but the others are silent.

'You probably think this is crazy,' she says, 'but he said I was the undertaker. I know it was a joke: but in a way it wasn't. I want to go to the grave and make it right.'

There is silence in the room.

'I wanted to know if one of you would show me where he is?'

The Mags is crying and John has his head in his hands. Sophie is staring into her tea.

Suddenly, the Mags stops crying and sits up straight.

'You are mad,' she says. 'Completely mad. And so am I. We'll both go.'

'You're not going anywhere without me,' says Sophie.

'What about you, John?' says the Mags.

'I'll stay here with the boys,' says young John. 'Look, I can see why you feel this way, but it's impossible. They put big concrete blocks over the grave,' he tells Sam. 'The sort they use at military check-points. They weigh a ton: you'll never move them.'

'I don't know what we'll do,' says Sam. 'All I know is that I'm going. I'll pour the stuff through the bloody cracks between the concrete blocks if I have to. But I'm going.'

'Well, it's too late to go now,' says John. 'Even if the police don't pick you up, you'll never get back before the curfew. Your best chance is very early in the morning.'

After Sam has gone there is a long silence.

'She's some undertaker,' says Sophie.

The strangest of days

It had rained steadily for two days but on the third morning the sky was clear. As they walked, the sunrise seemed to mock them in their despair. In less than a week the whole thing had plunged into disaster. Now they walked back to the grave, not knowing whether they, too, would be arrested.

They walked in silence, lost in their own thoughts. Finally they came to the place. There was no mistaking the two massive concrete blocks the Army had placed over the mouth of the grave to seal it. But as they approached the tomb they saw the heavy blocks had been moved aside.

The grave was open. And it was empty.

'It's the wrong grave,' said the Mags, pale with shock.

'With two concrete blocks? Just like you told me?' said Sam.

'It's the right grave: it's the only one cut into the hillside,' said Sophie. 'It's the right place but the body's been taken.'

'But who would take it? And how?' said Sam. 'You'd need a crane to move those blocks. In any case they're army property: no one would dare move them.'

'Who cares who moved them,' says the Mags. 'They've been moved and he's gone. That's all that matters.'

It was almost an hour later when they arrived back at the house. They told the others what had happened, but the boys seemed so chewed-up with their own problems they didn't believe them. While they have been away two of the gang have left, deciding it is too dangerous to stay. There was an argument, but they said they were going home, and that was it.

Now the Rox is furious with the three women for going off on their own. He says they must have gone to the wrong place.

'Why did you have to go back there? The last thing we want is to draw attention to ourselves. You want us all to end up dead?'

The Mags looks as though she is going to argue, but instead goes off to find a quiet place to grieve. But later, his words come back to her. Maybe they had gone to the wrong place.

For a long time she thinks about what has happened; and the more she thinks about it, the more confused she gets. Finally, without a word to the others, she sets off back to the grave.

When she gets to the place it's just as they left it. As the Mags looks inside I start to feel very uneasy: as though there is danger in the air. Maybe a hawk is circling around somewhere; but I can see nothing – unless he is keeping the sun behind him.

Then for some stupid reason the story of the great wings comes into my head, and I begin to think the sun is getting to me too. Or maybe I am just dreaming.

Suddenly, there comes a piercing scream from the Mags. I circle round, but nothing unusual seems to be going on. She is just talking to some guy who looks like he is a workman paid to tidy the graves.

But suddenly I realize I know this guy. Though I cannot believe it, I recognize him. It is the Boss.

The Mags is trying to hug him, but he is telling her something about the gang and to give them a message. He is laughing; and she is crying like her heart will break.

Then suddenly she takes off, back down the road into the city. I hesitate to follow her because I am still uneasy about the hawk and the strange feeling about the great wings; and so it is some time before I head back after her.

When I get there, a terrible row is raging. The Rox is yelling at her, and she is screaming at him; and the guys are shouting at both of them.

'No way did you see him,' roars the Rox. 'Absolutely no way. He is dead. We all know he is dead. You are hysterical.'

He stops for a moment, and then says something really strange: 'Anyway, I am the leader. He would have shown himself to me first. Not you. Not a woman.'

'Leader?' yells the Mags in fury. 'So where was the leader when they were nailing him up? Where were any of you?' she says turning on the rest of the guys, who suddenly go quiet. 'There were five of us there: five of us. And who were we? Four women and young John – that's who was there in the shit and the mud and the rain. Even the bloody sparrow was there. And where were you brave men? Hiding under a table in the cellar somewhere safe, that's where. Leader? Don't make me laugh.'

For a moment I think the Rox is going to strike her: sweat is pouring down his face which has gone blood red and he looks as though he wants to tear her apart. Instead he lets out a great roar of pain and goes crashing out of the house into the street.

There is silence. Then Andy says: 'Where's he gone?'

'To find the grave,' says young John. 'But he doesn't know where it is. I'd better show him.'

They are gone a long time and the gang are worried they have been picked up by the police; but finally they arrive back. The Rox is very quiet, as though he is worrying about something. As though there is bad news. But John is different – he's glowing with excitement.

Later he comes over and puts his arm round the Mags and they sit in silence. Finally she stops crying and he whispers: 'I think you were right.'

'About what?'

'About seeing the Boss.'

'What you mean is I'm going mad – like they said I was.'

'No. It only sounds crazy. But it isn't: maybe this is what it's all been about.'

'What's going to happen now?'

'I don't know.'

It is very late when there comes a thunderous hammering on the door. They know only too well who it will be: only the Army come banging on doors in the night.

But it is not the soldiers; it is the two men who decided to pack up and go home earlier in the day.

Food is found but it remains untouched as they tell their strange story.

They are on the bus heading north when some guy gets on and sits in the seat behind them. As they are going along, the man gets to talking with them. He is asking what has been happening in the city; and they say he must be the only person around who does not know what has been going on.

They tell him how the Boss is arrested and put on trial and then executed. The man sitting behind them is talking to them about something; but they are not really listening, because going over what has happened stirs up the pain and they are in despair.

When they finally get to their village, the stranger says he is going on further. But they tell him this is as far as the bus goes, and so he will have to walk to wherever it is he is going. Then they get to thinking this is not what the Boss would have said about generosity of spirit; and so they ask him to come and eat with them.

They are just sitting down to the meal, however, when the stranger takes a piece of the bread and breaks it. And suddenly they realize who he is.

There is silence. Then the Rox, who is getting irritated, says: 'And who is it?'

And one of the men says: 'It is the Boss.'

For a while everyone is shouting and talking at once. Finally there is quiet.

'So what happens then?' demands the Rox. 'Why have you not brought him with you? And, anyway, how did you get back at this time of night?'

'We jumped up from the table and went to find a taxi or someone to bring us back, but no one would risk going out during the curfew. When we got back into the house, the Boss was gone.'

'So what happened then?' says the Rox.

'Then we set off and walked back to the city, because we thought you would like to know the Boss is alive.'

'And we are tired with all this talking,' says the other one. 'And we have still not had our supper.'

Unmistaken identity

The death, when it came, had been sudden and terrible. Despite living with the fear of arrest for so long, the gang seemed completely unprepared for the speed and ferocity of what happened. Since then wild rumours, sparked off by the Mags and two of the others, have generated a mood of confusion and anxiety.

Finally some of the gang have left the city and headed north, back home to their boats; maybe hoping the familiar surroundings will ease the pain. But the old ways are not doing much to heal the wounds.

One evening the Rox announces. 'I'm sick of this. I'm going fishing.'

Four of them have been out on the lake all night without catching anything. Now they sit in silence in the early light of dawn; the mist clinging to their clothes. The water laps at the hull of the boat as they drift listlessly, resentful and silenced by their failure. Finally Andy stirs and picks up an oar. Tom does the same and, without a word, they pull slowly for the shore.

As the two men row, young John stands in the bow. He is watching a figure on the distant beach. Through the mist a man is waving; his voice drifts faintly across the water.

After a few moments young John turns to his companions: 'There's someone on the shore. He says there's fish on our starboard side. He says we should cast the net over there . . .'

'Tell him to get stuffed,' says a muffled voice from the stern where a large pair of buttocks in thick corduroy trousers are bending over a tangle of nets.

'Maybe he can see a shoal,' says Andy, as if the sudden appearance of fish could somehow take away their pain.

There is a rumble of frustration and rising anger from the stern as the Rox stands up, his face red from the exertion of struggling with useless nets. He turns and glares.

'Tell him to get lost. I don't need some idiot with a dog to tell me how to catch fish.'

'He hasn't got a dog,' says the younger man.

'They've always got a dog. Why else do they go for walks on the beach at this time in the morning?'

He makes his way to the front of the boat, his feet slipping on the wet planking. Joining young John in the bows, he squints across the water which is reflecting the first rays of the sun.

'Push off. And take your dog with you,' he shouts, his anger echoing emptily in the still morning air.

The man on the shore waves again and appears to do a little dance on the sand where he has lit a small fire.

'What the hell's he doing?' says the Rox.

'I think he's laughing at us.' says John,

'Idiot,' mutters the older man as he stumbles back to his nets.

There is a moment's indecision, then Tom says cautiously: 'Might as well give it a try.'

There is a murmur of agreement.

'Do what you like,' says the Rox sullenly. 'I'm having a fag.'

Seating himself on the gunwale of the boat, his backside precariously close to the water, he watches indifferently as his companions struggle to cast the net.

'Give us a hand,' says Tom, finally.

'Nuts,' says the Rox.

The three struggle for several more minutes, the sun increasingly hot on their backs. Eventually the Rox takes a final drag on the cigarette. He flicks the stub out over the water and steps across to his companions.

'Useless lot.'

Moments later the net is drifting out from the boat. They watch in silence as it sinks into the clear water, leaving only the yellow floats bobbing on the surface. For a long time they stand, each lost in their own thoughts as the wavelets slap gently against the hull.

Suddenly there is a movement and the line running out to the net snaps taut, sending a necklace of droplets showering into the water.

'A catch,' shouts Tom.

'A rock,' says the bigger man. 'You've snagged a rock.'

'It's not a rock, it's fish.'

'It's a rock. There are no fish.'

'Well, if it's a rock, it's moving.'

Without another word the four begin struggling with the net, which now seems to weigh more than the boat itself.

'Stop!' yells the Rox. 'You'll rip the blasted net. Just lash it to the boat and row for the shore. Slowly – we need to drag it into the shallows.'

As the boat is coaxed slowly towards the shore, young John resumes his position in the bows, scanning the beach.

Suddenly he turns back to his companions. 'Stop rowing,' he shouts. The men at the oars pause in mid-stroke, startled by the urgency in his voice. 'The man on the beach . . .'

'Well?'

'It's him. I'm certain. It's the Boss.'

Before he can say any more, there is an enormous splash as the Rox leaps fully clothed into the water, and vanishes.

The three peer over the side in time to see him break the surface and start splashing wildly towards the shore.

Young John shields his eyes against the sun and watches his progress.

'What's the man with the dog doing now?' asks Andy as he and his companion resume rowing.

'Sitting on the sand, watching the Rox . . . Now he's standing up. He's laughing at something.'

'Where's the Rox?'

'Staggering up the beach.'

'Now what's happening?'

'The Rox is talking to him. Now he's hugging him.'

'Is it the Boss?'

'Must be.'

The boat grounds gently on the beach.

As they walk up the shingle, the Boss calls out: 'Come and have breakfast.'

When they get there they see there are fish cooking on the fire.

'You're not the only ones who can catch fish,' says the Boss and laughs as he sees the look on their faces.

'This is how it all began,' says Andy.

'It's still beginning,' says the Boss. And over breakfast and into the morning he tells them what needs to be done. But he can see they are still in shock at coming face to face with him again.

'Don't worry so much,' he tells them. 'Relax. You believe in God – well, trust a bit more in me.

'If you love me you will do as I ask. Remember how bunches of grapes grow on the vines around here? The branches can't bear fruit unless they remain attached to the vine, can they? Well, just as the branch doesn't bear fruit by itself, neither can you unless you remain in me. It's not that difficult, is it?'

He looks round at their worried faces: 'Don't fret; I will not leave you desolate,' he says.

With all this churning round in their heads no one asks him how come he is here and not in the tomb. All they know is that the Mags and the others were telling the truth. That, or we are all mad. But this doesn't feel like madness; it feels like the first stirrings of new life.

Later the Boss and the Rox take a walk along the beach; maybe to sort a few things out. When they get back the Rox is very subdued. It seems unlikely this crew are going to do much by way of continuing the work the Boss has been doing. Telling people they are loved by God is one thing; but telling people that God loves the poor is another.

And telling people that God wants justice and respect for every person on the planet, because they are all his children, sounds like trouble. As they have found out over the past few days.

Finally, the Boss says he needs to be moving on but he will see them again. And when they are left alone on the beach, I have to say that, while I love these guys dearly, they do not inspire me with confidence.

The counter-attack

Few things are more dangerous than a wounded animal. You'd think it would run away and hide but, instead, its instinct for survival erupts in a sudden determination to fight back. Just when its adversary expects it to withdraw to allow its wounds to heal, it turns and attacks with renewed ferocity.

On the surface little seems to have changed in the life of Mr Mammon. He is in a somewhat sombre mood; though why this should be so is a mystery, since everything has gone well for him over the past few weeks. Thanks to careful crowd management, the execution took place as planned; though there were people who said the prisoner looked half-dead by the time he was strung up.

The trouble-maker who had been saying unhelpful things about wealth and possessions is dead and gone. So Mr Mammon and his trans-global organization should be pleased with the way things have turned out.

But for some reason they are not. Mr Mammon has the strange feeling he has been here before. For a start, there is a rumour going round that the trouble-maker they executed is still alive. By the sound of it, even more alive than he was before. His friends and hangers-on, who at first went into hiding, are suddenly to be seen around the city.

The army detail who handled the execution have been called in and questioned at length; but they are positive the prisoner was dead. In fact the soldier who was sent to make sure, says the body was already changing – as happens after death. But to make absolutely certain, he plunged his bayonet deep into the corpse. He felt the blade tear into the vital organs. If there is one thing this soldier is good at, it is making sure people are dead. And this guy was definitely dead.

So why does every instinct tell Mr Mammon that something is wrong? As though he himself has received a terrible injury, and his trans-world enterprise is threatened?

Something has happened. Silently and unseen, everything has changed; though he cannot work out where the danger is coming from. One thing is for certain, however: the rag-bag group who were with the trouble-maker must be neutralized.

As he struggles to find an answer, he becomes aware of a fly buzzing at the window. Mr Mammon jumps to his feet: the fly has not been seen for a long time. But, when he gets over to the window, he sees it is just an ordinary house fly.

Meanwhile, in another part of the city, the gang are also unhappy today. The growing confidence of the last few weeks has given way to anxiety and despair. The reason is that the Boss is saying it is time for him to be moving on permanently, He keeps telling them not to be afraid and that he will be with them in spirit; but they do not take much comfort from this.

The Rox in particular is in despair at the idea of the Boss not being around. Young John tries to comfort him: 'If you were going on a plane journey, would you want the pilot sitting with the passengers, or somewhere out of sight flying the aircraft?' he says. The Rox grumbles that is a stupid idea, but at least it's got him thinking.

Finally, the Boss tells them it is time for them to part. Those who are still around get up very early one morning and set off with him into the country. At first it is just the Mags and Sophie and the boys, but soon other people hear something is going on and, before long, there are a couple of dozen others there as well.

The Boss leads them out onto a hillside. The Mags is in tears and young John and the boys are also upset. They are telling the Boss they love him; but even now he is not letting them get away with being sentimental. He reminds them that those who love him are those who do what he says.

'Those who love me are they who hear my commandments and keep them. Just remember,' he tells them, 'the word you hear is not mine but that of the Father who sent me.'

No matter what happens, he says, he will be with them as they go out and tell people about the love of God. The love that shows itself in justice and respect for all people: especially the poor. A love which is nothing less than the gift of life itself.

As he is talking no one seems to notice the mist forming on the hillside. Or maybe it is low cloud. Anyway, as he stops speaking, the mist rolls in and for a few minutes the crowd are wrapped in the soft, cool vapour.

When it finally clears, the Boss is gone, and we never see him again. Though sometimes, when you see a homeless guy begging in the street or a hungry child on the TV, you get the feeling he is somewhere very close.

The gang head back into town and I would like to say that they were in high spirits. But, to be truthful, many of them are totally broken up by the realization that this was the final parting.

Maybe it was for comfort, but they often met together to talk about what had happened. Usually their meetings were in secret; for fear that they, too, would be arrested. The word on the street was that there was likely to be a crack-down on dissident groups. Especially known associates of the Boss.

Some of the gang were for splitting up and going to different towns and villages, but the Rox said the Boss had been quite clear: they were to wait in the city. But for what, he did not know.

Then, one day when they are all together, something happens that changes the whole thing. As though the sun has unexpectedly burst through thick clouds.

The way I heard it, they were all filled with a new mood of confidence and hope. Amazingly, they were not afraid any more. Instead of staying in hiding in case they were arrested, they were out in the streets talking to people about the Boss and the love of God and freedom and justice for the poor.

Naturally, the authorities are not going to allow this to happen and suddenly they strike back. One of the gang, a young guy called Stephen, is arrested and beaten up so badly that he dies. But, even though this is shocking, it does not stop the gang. In fact the killing has a strange effect. It turns out that, even when Stephen is being beaten up, he does not seem to be afraid.

The rumour is that, as he is dying, he is still talking about the love of God; and this has a deep effect on all who hear the story.

It certainly has a profound effect on Mr Mammon when word gets back to him. For a long time he is silent as though tormented by a terrible doubt. Although he does not show it, there is a rising anger in him. For weeks he cannot think of a way to attack his unseen adversary. For some reason, his primary weapon – of instilling fear into people – no longer seems to work. And if you cannot make people afraid, what can you do? You cannot kill everybody.

Mrs Mammon makes him a cup of coffee and is very sympathetic and they sit for a long time in silence. As he sits, a strange picture is forming in Mr Mammon's mind. For some reason he is thinking about a man dying of thirst in the desert. Suddenly he laughs out loud. But it is not a pleasant sound. It is more like the snarl of triumph as a wounded animal turns on its attacker.

'What is it?' asks his wife.

'It is the answer,' he says quietly. 'The way to strike back. We need to be subtle. It's no good meeting this thing head on. No matter how many of them we kill, it will make no difference. The Army can try, but it won't work.'

Mrs Mammon looks puzzled: 'So what's the plan?'

'Money – it's always the answer. Instead of arresting them, we bank-roll them.'

'Are you crazy?' says Mrs Mammon in alarm.

'Not crazy. Inspired. We will give them money – more money than they have ever seen. We will praise them, flatter them and make them powerful. We will place our own people among them.'

'And?'

'We sit back and watch. Gradually they will begin to want other things. Titles and fine robes. They will want their own buildings. Great buildings. They will have wealth and power. The leaders of the world will want to join them. And use them.'

'You think that will work?'

'Absolutely. We destroy them from within. They will gradually forget the man who came out of the desert and told them about the love and justice of God and freedom for the poor. They will be the new Robed Ones.'

'But not all of them will forget.'

'No, you are right. Some will struggle on. A few perhaps; they will stay true. But as they work for justice, we will sow greed and envy; as they try to bring dignity and respect, we will spread prejudice and hate; as they talk of faith and trust, we will create fear and suspicion. They will be the minority — a pathetic remnant looked down upon by the others. The ones who want an easy life.

'What did the man say? "You cannot serve both God and Mammon." Well, I know which most of them will choose.'

The promise

And that was how it all began. It seems strange, looking back on those few short years with the Boss. He was not rich or powerful but the Spirit of God was in him. He was the chosen one: the one in whom God delights. The one who shows us the nature and purpose of God. The one who reveals what it is to be truly human.

And the gang? He loved them to the end – and beyond. 'I am with you always,' he said, 'until the end of time.'

And the promise was to all of them: men, women – even a sparrow. And if a sparrow, maybe also you.

And Mr Mammon with his trans global empire: what happened to him? Look around at what is going on in the world. But even with all his wealth and power, he cannot destroy what the Boss has started; because it is the affirmation of life itself.

The Spirit of God that will not rest until there is justice over all the earth.

And what greater adventure – than to be part of that?